SO, YOU WANT TO BE A LAWYER, EH?

SO, YOU WANT TO BE A LAWYER, EH?

A Comprehensive Guidebook for Prospective and Current Canadian Law Students

Adam Letourneau, B.Sc., B.A., LL.B.

Writing On Stone Press

ISBN 0-9738092-0-5

Writing on Stone Press Inc.
www.writingonstone.ca
www.CanadaLawStudent.ca
info@CanadaLawStudent.ca

For my children, Zoë, Soleil and Zane.

May you reach every big goal you set.

TABLE OF CONTENTS

INTRODUCTION 1

A. WHY THIS BOOK NEEDED TO BE WRITTEN OR WHY I
WROTE THIS BOOK 1
B. WHAT QUALIFIES THE AUTHOR TO WRITE THIS BOOK?. 2
C. COMPREHENSIVE CANADIAN LAW STUDENTS' GUIDE... 3
D. THE ULTIMATE CANADIAN LAW SCHOOL SOURCE 4
E. OPINION COUNTS 4
F. ACKNOWLEDGMENTS 4

CHAPTER 1: WHAT DOES THE ROAD LOOK LIKE?
.... 5

A. REASONS FOR APPLYING TO LAW SCHOOL? 5
   a. Finances, Pay, Underemployment, etc. 8
   b. Status... 8
B. GRUELLING, VERY COMPETITIVE, BUT REWARDING 8
C. CHALLENGING JOB MARKET 10
D. DO I WANT TO TRAVEL THAT ROAD? 10
E. STATISTICS – HOW MANY LAWYERS ARE THERE? 12
F. HOW MANY APPLY? HOW MANY ARE ACCEPTED? 12
G. LSAT AND GPA STATS 14
H. WHAT IS LAW SCHOOL LIKE ANYWAY? 15

CHAPTER 2: HOW DO I PASS THE LSAT? 17

A. PREP COURSES 19
B. BOOKS 20
C. CD-ROMS 22
D. STRATEGIES 22
E. TRY, TRY AGAIN! 23
F. DO NOT SHARE YOUR SCORE WITH ANYBODY! 23

CHAPTER 3: THE APPLICATION PROCESS........... 25

A. WHICH SCHOOL? 25
   a. Rankings – Do They Mean Anything? 26
   b. Rising Tuition Costs! 30

    c. Considerations *32*
    d. Should I Look South? *32*
    e. Special Status – Mature and Aboriginal Students ... *33*
  B. LL.B. VS. JD 37
  C. COMBINED PROGRAMS 38
    a. MBA/LL.B. *40*
    b. B.C.L./LL.B. *43*
  D. ACTUAL PROCESS OF APPLYING TO LAW SCHOOL 43
    a. Admissions Information and FAQ's *43*
    b. Strategies *45*
    c. Résumé *46*
    d. References – What Kind are Best? *47*
    e. Deadlines, etc. *48*
    f. Deferral *48*

CHAPTER 4: FIRST YEAR (1L) **51**

  A. HOW TO HANDLE THE LOAD 51
    a. Time Management *51*
  B. THE SOCIAL ASPECT – JR. HIGH AGAIN 57
  C. FIRST YEAR SUBJECTS (SCHOOL BY SCHOOL) 61
  D. EXTRACURRICULAR ACTIVITIES 65
  E. GRADES, GRADES, GRADES – OR, DOES IT MATTER? 67
  F. EXAM WRITING STRATEGIES 69
  G. LEGAL RESEARCH AND WRITING – STRATEGIES 70
  H. SEEK OUT A REAL MENTOR 72
  I. TO WORK PART TIME OR NOT? 73
  J. THE BILLS ARE COMING – HOW DO I KEEP UP? 74
  K. AVOID LAW SCHOOL TUNNEL VISION 76
  L. 1L ATTITUDE AND BEHAVIOUR TIPS: 78
    a. In Class Comments *78*
    b. Sense of Humour *79*
    c. Share Your Notes! *81*
    d. Don't Share Grades – Period *82*
    e. Keep Your Opinions to Yourself *83*
  M. 1L MOOT 83
    a. Strategies to Prepare for the Moot *84*
    b. How to Compose Yourself *87*

   c. The Debrief *89*
N. FINDING A SUMMER JOB 90
O. THE CANADIAN BAR ASSOCIATION (CBA) 98
P. EXECUTIVE POSITIONS IN LAW SCHOOL 98
Q. REGISTERING FOR 2L COURSES WHILE STILL IN 1L 99
R. ADVICE FROM 2LS AND 3LS 103
S. STUDENT LEGAL SERVICES 104
T. DO I NEED A LAPTOP? 107
U. TEXTBOOKS – USED? NEW? 111
V. PRO BONO WORK 111
W. STUDY HABITS 112
   a. Reading Textbooks *113*
X. APPLY FOR 1L SUMMER JOB 118
Y. CANNING! 119
   a. Do Your Own CAN! *120*
   b. Three Kinds of CANS *121*
   c. Commercial Cans *124*
   d. Online Resources *125*
Z. PRACTICE EXAMS 127
AA. STUDY GROUPS 129
BB. EXERCISE – SO IMPORTANT! 131
CC. ACCOMMODATIONS – RESOURCES 132
DD. EXAM WRITING STRATEGIES 134
   a. IRAC (Issue, Ratio, Analysis, Conclusion) *136*
   b. Don't Be Too Eloquent *138*
   c. Approach Your Instructor *138*
   d. It's All About Getting as Many Points as Possible *139*
EE. 1L EVALUATION 141

CHAPTER 5: SUMMER JOB **143**

A. OPTIONS 143
   a. Firm *143*
   b. Internship *148*
   c. Corporate *148*
   d. Research for Professor *150*
   e. Student Legal Services *151*
B. WHAT ELSE CAN I DO WITH MY 1L SUMMER? 152

a. Study Abroad? *152*
b. Get Away from Law? Travel *152*
C. NETWORK! 153
D. HOW TO WRITE YOUR FIRST MEMO 154
E. WHY AM I DOING DELIVERIES? 156
F. MAKE AN IMPRESSION 158
G. DO THE WORK YOU WANT TO DO 159
H. ACCEPT AN ARTICLE OFFER OR NOT? 160
I. SCHOLARSHIP APPLICATIONS 162

CHAPTER 6: SECOND YEAR (2L) 163

A. MARKS, MARKS, MARKS? 163
B. LAW REVIEW 165
C. MOOTING PROGRAMS 167
D. RESEARCH FOR ARTICLES – COMPARING FIRMS 172
E. CAREER DAY 176
F. THE KILLER RÉSUMÉ 176
a. Personal Web Site? *178*
G. APPLYING FOR COURT CLERKSHIPS 180
H. APPLYING FOR 2L SUMMER JOB 189

CHAPTER 7: SECOND SUMMER 191

A. WHAT SUMMER JOB IS BEST? 191
B. ARTICLE APPLICATION PROCESS 192
a. Timing *192*
b. Application Packages *193*
c. Multiple Cities? *194*
d. Hidden Rural Gems *195*
e. Match Program *201*
f. Scheduling Interviews *202*
g. Phone Message *204*
h. Cell Phone? *204*
i. What to Wear *205*
j. Interviewing *209*
k. Be Yourself *212*
l. Prepare *216*
m. Ask the Right Questions *217*

n. Reveal Intentions 218
o. Try to be Honest 220
p. Bow Out When Appropriate 221
q. The Thank You Letter 221
r. Call-Back Interviews 223
s. The Witching Hour 223
t. Accepting an Offer 224
C. SCHOLARSHIP APPLICATIONS 226

CHAPTER 8: THIRD YEAR (3L) 227

A. WHAT CLASSES? 227
B. MOOTS? 229
C. PASS/FAIL COURSES 229
D. RESEARCH PAPERS? 230
E. WHAT TO DO IF YOU DIDN'T GET AN ARTICLE (YET) ... 232
F. ARE GRADES STILL IMPORTANT? 234
G. CHECK CREDIT AND COURSE REQUIREMENTS 236
H. HELP OUT THOSE BELOW YOU 236
I. OPPORTUNITIES FOR NON FACULTY CLASSES 237
J. REGISTER FOR BAR EXAM COURSES / CPLED 237
K. ARRANGE START DATE FOR YOUR ARTICLE 238
L. 3L EVALUATION 238

CHAPTER 9: CONCLUSION & FINAL THOUGHTS 241

APPENDICES 243

A. ALTERNATIVE CAREERS FOR LAWYERS 243
B. LAW SCHOOL ADMISSION INFORMATION 244
C. SAMPLE COVER LETTERS AND SAMPLE RÉSUMÉ 245
D. SAMPLE STATEMENTS OF INTEREST 253
E. LAW LINKS 258
F. LAW SCHOOLS IN CANADA 259

ABOUT THE AUTHOR 263

INTRODUCTION

Law is king of all.
— Henry Alford

A. WHY THIS BOOK NEEDED TO BE WRITTEN OR WHY I WROTE THIS BOOK

So, you want to be a lawyer, eh? In 2001, I began the formal journey towards becoming a lawyer. I was as green as they come. I had made the decision that I wanted to take a shot at law school. Now what? I was lost. I started my research using the Internet, and by calling various law schools across Canada. After a gruelling double attempt at the LSAT, and after a lot of sifting and seeking out information from anybody and everybody that I knew connected to law, I was finally able to complete my applications to law school. Then after months of eager anticipation, I gained acceptance into the fold. Although this was a difficult and confusing procedure, it was only a taste of what law school had to offer in terms of challenges, obstacles and sessions of hair pulling.

As I approached the end of the law school journey and embarked upon the practical field of law, I often wished that I had obtained a guide to succeeding in law school. I read a lot of American "guidebooks," which offered some introductory information about what law school was all about, but I have wished for a guidebook that contained the information that was really applicable and useful to the Canadian law student. I never did find that guidebook, so I decided to write it myself. It is my hope that the contents of this book will help you in your decision to enter the field of law, help you gain entrance into law school, and in particular, help you to succeed in law school and beyond.

B. WHAT QUALIFIES THE AUTHOR TO WRITE THIS BOOK?

Right from the moment that I decided to apply for law school, my life has been non-stop information gathering. I do not mind admitting that I have become a compulsive law-related information junkie. I have pored over law school rankings, law firm rankings, law firm websites, articling pamphlets, etc. I have also been incredibly interested in what law graduates are doing with their education, reading whatever articles that I can get a hold of related to law graduate career choices.

So, with all of this information swimming around in my head, it seemed natural to make it available to others following the same path. Here is a real-life chance to help others, one of the aspirations of all future lawyers, and I am jumping on it. I am excited about my career in law, am thankful for the opportunity, and feel satisfied in the choices that I have made so far. I made those choices only after thoroughly scanning the horizon, which was really a lot of work! I received many interviews for articling positions and received a good number of offers from some very prestigious firms. I believe that I have a lot of expertise that I can share with you about how to get that elusive and cherished first job in law. I feel that I hold a very wide range of experience in law school, from academics to extracurricular activity to summer jobs to articling. I sincerely hope that you accept the information contained in this book eagerly and that it helps you in your mission to succeed in your journey through law school and beyond. I hope that it saves you time and that you will share the knowledge with your colleagues.

C. COMPREHENSIVE CANADIAN LAW STUDENTS' GUIDE

This is the first of hopefully many editions of this guidebook. As a result, it is a work in progress. I plan to update the information contained in the pages of this book yearly, resulting in the most comprehensive guidebook for the Canadian law student available.

In this book, you will find personal anecdotes, both from the author and from colleagues of the author. As well, you will find the most in-depth research and information about law schools in Canada, the application process, law school study habits, summer jobs, the articling process, and more.

No guidebook can cover everything. The law and legal education are big topics. Further, it is not always easy to understand the subtle differences between Canadian law schools. If you feel that you can add any information, or think that I should be including information particular to a certain law school or region, please let me know and I will include that information in the next edition of this book. I will also make sure that such information is accessible in the meantime on the website www.canadalawstudent.ca.

To send me your comments, suggestions or criticisms, please email me at adam@canadalawstudent.ca and I will get back to you as soon as possible.

You will also find other useful information at www.canadalawstudent.ca, including law links, links to online CANS/outlines (condensed annotated notes – basically, a summary of what you have learned in the term – more about these later), prospective and current law student surveys on important questions facing these groups and more.

D. THE ULTIMATE CANADIAN LAW SCHOOL SOURCE

If you find any information contained within this book to be inaccurate, outdated or misguiding, please contact me immediately at adam@canadalawstudent.ca. By doing so, you will ensure that your colleagues will have the information that they need to succeed. All updates that you provide, along with updates researched by the author, will be added to subsequent editions of this guidebook.

E. OPINION COUNTS

To augment the material in this book, I have asked a number of classmates and colleagues to answer a number of key questions about their law school application, law school experience, and about landing a job. I include answers to these questions throughout as A Word from the Wise . I chose students or graduates of law school who I thought were examples of success. I have also included a section written by a colleague who is much more knowledgeable and experienced with the topic of applying for court clerkships.

F. ACKNOWLEDGMENTS

I would like to first thank my wife, Carmen, for her emotional and intellectual support through law school and for editing this book. If it were legal to have her added to my LL.B. parchment, I would arrange to have it done in a heartbeat. She deserves the degree as much as I do. I would also like to thank my test readers, Shawn and Maiko Davis, along with the contributors to A Word from the Wise that are interspersed in this book. Your support is greatly appreciated.

CHAPTER 1: WHAT DOES THE ROAD LOOK LIKE?

*Law school taught me one thing: how to take two situations
that are exactly the same and show how they are different.*
— Hart Pomerantz

A. REASONS FOR APPLYING TO LAW SCHOOL?

Every law student or lawyer to whom I have posed the question, "What made you decide on law school?" has provided a different answer. There are literally thousands of reasons for embarking on this new career. I have heard of people who wrote the LSAT on a dare, who have done it because they love lawyer movies and TV shows, or who found inspiration in a court case that they read about in the newspaper. I have heard people say that they felt that they had no choice – that nothing else looked good. I often hear people say (some sheepishly and some aggressively) that the money attracted them. Others have indicated that they like the idea of power, prestige and wearing a pinstripe suit on Bay Street. I have heard many times that the reason was that they wanted to help others. There is no right reason or wrong reason. However, there must be a compelling personal reason.

For me, law was a real career change. Before applying to law school, I was Vice President of Operations for an electronic publishing house that specialized in travel and outdoor activity guidebooks for your Personal Digital Assistant or PDA (i.e. Palm, Pocket PC). The idea was that you could bring along all of your cumbersome guidebooks in your pocket-sized PDA while backpacking or cycling or traveling. It was a fantastic job, always putting me on the cutting edge of Internet and computer technology. However, I was ready for new challenges, and the Internet and technology fields had already dropped from their incredible peak in popularity and economic skyrocketing. My body was suffering from being in front of a computer for hours at a time – I had repetitive strain in my wrists, back and legs. So after raising tons of money and making huge progress, our company looked like it was about to fizzle out. It was the perfect time to jump on an opportunity that I had been considering for some time. I read an article that suggested that the best time to embark on further education was during a downtime in the economy. I did not need much more incentive. I signed up for the LSAT exam, and found myself suffering along with a couple of hundred other students in a large auditorium. My desire to succeed was evidenced by my terror – a feeling that lasted until I was finally accepted into law school.

A Word from the Wise – Practical Experience

For me, going to law school was more accident than plan. As I was finishing my first degree, I was not sure what I wanted to do, but I knew I wanted a change. Studying law seemed like it would be both an intellectual challenge and something with a direct practical application, so I decided to try it.
— Robin Penker, University of Alberta

I thought that no matter what I chose to do in the future, a law degree would provide a great foundation. One can do so many things with a legal background — e.g. teach, open up a business, work as in-house counsel for a company, etc.
— Kim Yee, University of Alberta

I was always interested in law. I really enjoyed writing and argumentation. I thought law would be a good degree to have regardless of what I ended up doing.

— Mike Kariya, University of Calgary

Law school has always been a lifelong dream. I was inspired by the thought of advocating for others in addition to participating in large business transactions.
— Rob Nelson, Queen's University, University of Calgary transfer student

I wanted to go to law school for a number of years before starting my post-secondary education…I chose to apply to law school mainly because I felt unsatisfied with my current education and couldn't see myself working in the field that I was studying.
— Jamie Johnson, University of Alberta

I had always wanted to go to law school. It was probably in grade 9 that I decided I wanted to go to law school, because of my interest in social studies and politics. In fact, in grade nine I had to write a paper about my career goals and to describe some goals and steps to get there. So at that point, I researched and learned a lot about how to apply and what I needed to go to law school. After my first degree in Arts, I decided to work for a while in Edmonton (where I am from). After working for about eight months (and after applying to law schools in western Canada), I was offered an opportunity of a lifetime - to work on Parliament Hill in Ottawa (a dream job for a Poli Sci grad). I then moved to Ottawa and after a year and a bit of working there and an issue of job security, I decided to look back to my original goal of attending law school and so reapplied to some schools and considered some deferrals I had at other schools.
— Lorne Randa, University of Alberta

I had completed a three-year contract job. I wanted to embark upon a career. Truthfully, I somewhat romanticized the profession of law and did not know nearly as much as I should have about what lawyers do before applying to law school.
— Shawn Davis, University of Calgary LLB/MBA

a. Finances, Pay, Underemployment, etc.

As you read this book, you will find that law is not all roses. One of the most popular reasons for entering law is because of the potential for a high personal income. It *is* possible to make good money as a lawyer. It *is* true that lawyers are at the upper end in terms of annual income and bonuses in Canada and the U.S. These are not terrible reasons to enter the law. Although annual salaries are very high for some lawyers, if you were to break down the hourly income for many lawyers compared to others, you might be surprised. This is especially true for junior and mid-level lawyers who are striving for that pot-of-gold called partnership. I will address the daily life of a lawyer in a later chapter.

b. Status

Contrary to many jokes and popular belief, one of the most prevalent reasons for becoming a lawyer is that the professional designation of being a lawyer brings with it prestige and in some cases, power. If this is important to you, law is probably a good choice. Lawyers are trusted members of the community that often carry the appearance of prestige and power. However, note that prestige and power can be dangerous in large quantities.

B. GRUELLING, VERY COMPETITIVE, BUT REWARDING

> *Pursue your passion and live your dream.*
> — Katherine Logan

Law school is hard. There are a few super-human individuals who will argue that they slid through law school unscathed. Nevertheless, for most mere mortals, law school is just plain hard. It is time-intensive, extremely competitive, and the material is often new and challenging. It is my hope that this guidebook will assist you with the challenge of seeing clearly.

You may have heard stories about law students putting in 12-14 hour days or more. You may have heard about students who have hidden library books before exam time, or about students who have deliberately tried to throw off fellow students before exam time. While these things do happen, for many the overall experience is very rewarding, filled with camaraderie and teamwork. The feelings of self-worth that come with grasping a legal concept, nailing a law exam or winning a moot competition are incalculable, and make all of the hours spent studying and preparing well worth the effort.

A Word from the Wise – Practical Experience

What makes a good lawyer?
Big Firm: time management, ability to consistently bill hours at a tepid pace, ability to meet competing expectations thrown at you from multiple directions, having a spouse/significant other who is eternally understanding.
Small Firm (fewer than 10 lawyers): all the same as big firm but billable hours usually not as earth shatteringly important.
— Shawn Davis, University of Calgary LLB/MBA

What makes a good lawyer? This is a tough question, because this really depends on the type of law one wishes to practice. In some areas, people skills are essential, in others, being aggressive and outgoing is key, and in others being passive and calm is needed. Overall however, any good lawyer requires the ability to think analytically, listen well and be able to pull out relevant information. A good lawyer is also one with strong research skills (which law schools also teach) and the ability to communicate well, whether it be orally or in written form.
— Lorne Randa, University of Alberta

C. CHALLENGING JOB MARKET

Current lawyers and personal research tell that there was a time when most law students could obtain a law article position. Today, there are far fewer articling positions available relative to the numbers of graduates, with numbers dwindling over the last decade. It is common to have 30-40% of second year law students exit the articling summer without articles lined up. Frightening as this may be, like the LSAT and the law school admission process, the articling application process is another opportunity to weed out those students who are not up to the standard required of a very demanding career.

With that thought, however, I believe that there will always be a need for lawyers. There will always be legal work. If you work hard, and have a sincere desire to be a lawyer, you will succeed and will end up finding a job in the field. If you follow the strategies outlined in this guidebook, you may even love your end position.

D. DO I WANT TO TRAVEL THAT ROAD?

Like all important decisions, it is important to take stock and to analyze the pros and cons before embarking upon a new path. Law school is not for everybody. It is a huge commitment in terms of time and money, along with emotional energy. I would encourage you to really think about the decision and write down all of the pros and cons for you personally. Talk to as many people as you can about your decision. Talk to any significant partners, friends or parents about the decision. For me, it was useful to envision what it would be like to be a lawyer. What emotions were attached to that vision? Could I imagine myself dressed up in a suit? In court? Defending a murderer? Making a big deal in a large corporation? Dealing with prisoners? Caught in the middle of a fighting couple in a divorce? Could I imagine myself preparing for a case or a settlement?

Note: Writing these things down may be important to lift you up later when you feel discouraged or overwhelmed.

A Word from the Wise – Practical Experience

Talk to current law school students, articling students, junior associates, and don't always believe the propaganda on the websites of the large firms. Also, consider other careers and whether the skyrocketing law tuition costs will be reasonable vis-à-vis the credentials you obtain.
— Shawn Davis, University of Calgary LLB/MBA

Make sure that you have done your research into the legal profession. Know what you're getting into. Law school is too much hard work to do for three years and then decide that the profession is not what you thought it would be
— Mike Kariya, University of Calgary

Many people are not fit for law school; you really, really need to understand the dedication necessary to succeed in law school. You need to have a lot of humility (there is no room for arrogance) and you need to understand that you may be disappointed. Law school is not for the faint of heart – getting into law school and being in law school are two different things. You need to crave it, fixate on it and have a passion for it or you won't succeed.
— Gayle Hiscocks, University of Calgary

Be very sure that law school is something that you really want; otherwise, it could prove to be an arduous process.
— Rob Nelson, Queen's University, University of Calgary transfer student

E. STATISTICS – HOW MANY LAWYERS ARE THERE?

The Federation of Law Societies of Canada puts out statistics on Canadian Lawyers each year. The last available set of statistics is from 2002. 2003 and 2004 should be available soon. You can get full access to all statistics at http://www.flsc.ca/en/lawsocieties/statisticslinks.asp.

As of 2002, there were around 54,000 practicing, insured member lawyers in Canada, broken down into 16,746 females and 37,127 males. There were actually almost 86,000 lawyers in Canada if you count practicing members exempt from insurance, non-resident practicing members, and non-practicing members.

If you look carefully at these statistics,[1] you will find a few interesting things. The first item of note is the relatively high number of sole practitioners in most provinces. The second thing is the decreasing number of lawyers as you progress through years as a member of the bar. Evidently, there are not so many runners at mile 20 as there were at the starting line.

You will find some other very interesting information provided for each province and territory such as: how many law firms (of various sizes) there are, admission rates to articles and calls to the bar, average practicing fees, insurance coverage, complaint rates, and full contact information for law societies in each province.

F. HOW MANY APPLY? HOW MANY ARE ACCEPTED?

You will see details in Appendix B on the number of applications and the number of spots available at each law school in Canada. There is a large discrepancy across the

---

[1] http://www.flsc.ca/en/pdf/statistics2002.pdf.

country. Many prospective law students are curious about where they may have the best chance of gaining acceptance. The number of spots and the number of admissions are not clearly indicative of your chance for success. It is important to consider other information, such as the average GPA and average LSAT for incoming students. It is also useful to inquire of each law school that you apply to what the percentage of in-province and out-of-province applications they accept on a percentage basis. This information is not included in this book, but will be readily available from the admissions office at the respective school where you apply.

Another consideration for prospective law students is to realize that the numbers in the Appendix B spreadsheet can be misleading. There is a lot of crossover between applications at the various schools. There are also a relatively large number of acceptance letters sent out each year, with many students declining offers. The truth is that most prospective students apply to multiple schools. Those at the top of the heap will gain acceptance at more than one school. However, they can only attend one school, and so must turn down one or more offers. This forces the schools to move down their list until they have all of their positions filled.

Apply to more than one law school. Apply to as many as possible, within your guidelines for location, school prestige, school offerings and tuition. It is surprising to hear how many students are accepted to more than one school. On the other hand, I am aware of students who only applied to one law school. I would advise against this, as the odds will not favour you. Personally, I applied to four law schools and was accepted at three.

All prospective students should put their all into every application that they put out. Those students who believe they may be closer to the middle of the pack should put even more into their applications. Make sure that there is nothing that would cause an admissions officer to put your application into the reject pile. **No spelling errors, nothing missing, all signatures included, and a smashing personal letter will all give you an advantage over those less careful. Every spot has to be filled in every law school. Make sure that you give yourself every advantage that you can to ensure success.**

G. LSAT AND GPA STATS

Law schools are looking for the best. Most admissions offices believe that the LSAT is a good indicator of future potential as a law student, and ultimately as a lawyer. Different law schools give the LSAT score more or less weight compared with the GPA. See the chart in Appendix B to see the LSAT/GPA ratios of different law schools. When you write your LSAT, you will be given a raw score as well as a percentile score. For those of you who are unfamiliar with percentile scores, they basically work like this: If you are in the 75th percentile that means that you scored higher or equal to 75% of those who have written the LSAT. That includes many people! It is important that you know what the average LSAT score is for each school that you apply to, whether in raw score or percentile form. Also, become aware of what the minimum LSAT score was last year, and any other information that you can get from the admissions officer about what the matrix of LSAT and GPA scores for the previous entering class was. This matrix will provide you with a more accurate scope of what kind of students the school is letting in and where you might fit into such a matrix. It will differ from school to school.

Most schools will look at your last two years of undergraduate work for your considered GPA. There are some subtle nuances between each school, and you should become very familiar with these to give yourself the most advantage in the application process.

H. WHAT IS LAW SCHOOL LIKE ANYWAY?

This is a very good question to ask if you are considering becoming a lawyer. Law school has a very different atmosphere from most other undergraduate and graduate programs out there. It has an extremely high workload, and is peculiarly competitive. This book is a great place to start to get a feel for what law school is really like. I explore some of the social aspects, some of the type of work, and many of the challenges that you will face in law school. You will find that throughout this book, I try to be as honest as possible about what law school is really like. I try not to take the all-too-common pessimistic viewpoint, but rather try to look at the process of becoming a lawyer in a positive manner.

Law school is not for everybody. Nevertheless, if after reading this book, and after consulting with a number of people already involved in the legal community, you decide that it is for you, you may find yourself immersed in the most challenging, most rewarding experience of your life.

CHAPTER 2: HOW DO I PASS THE LSAT?

For many persons, law appears to be black magic—an obscure domain that can be fathomed only by the professional initiated into the mysteries.
— Susan C. Ross

There are many books and articles devoted entirely to this subject. This chapter will give you an overview of the important information and point you to places where you can go to learn more.

According to informal surveys, most people write the LSAT more than once. Some say that rewriting will not significantly improve your score. In my case however, my second try resulted in a marked improvement. After my first poor showing, I then took a personal inventory of how I had prepared the first time and came up with a methodology that I was sure worked for me. I have heard this same strategy for others who have had to write the LSAT more than once. I found strategies that allowed me to more fully comprehend the games section of the LSAT, which brought my scores up considerably on the practice exams, which I dedicated myself to the second time around.

On my second attempt, I received a score that was well within the acceptable range for law schools in Canada. I was terrified that the first score would ruin my chances to gain acceptance, but I was accepted to three out of four law schools that I applied to.

A Word from the Wise – Practical Experience

I completed three practice exams under strict time constraints. I used an alarm clock and allowed myself one minute less than normally allowed on each section.
— Shawn Davis, University of Calgary LLB/MBA

I took the Renert tutorial course and practiced in my third year of undergrad twice per week for three months.
— Gayle Hiscocks, University of Calgary

To prepare for the LSAT, I purchased a study guidebook with CD ROM and obtained as many old LSAT exams as I could. From there I relied on the guidebook to practice strategies for answering questions and then practiced writing as many exams as I could in exam-like situations (i.e. timed sessions). I did this about two to three months before writing the actual exam.
— Lorne Randa, University of Alberta

To prepare for the LSAT I went online to the LSAC website and ordered a number of different practice LSATs from previous years. I spent the Saturdays for the last month before the LSAT by timing myself and taking the practice tests. Other than the practice test I only went through the LSAC website and read different hints and suggestions that were available.
— Jaime Johnson, University of Alberta

I took an LSAT prep course and completed lots of practice exams.
— Rob Nelson, Queen's University, University of Calgary transfer student

Law School Admission Council (LSAC):
http://www.lsac.org/.

A. Prep Courses

Many prospective law students feel more confident going into the LSAT having taken a preparatory course. Kaplan and The Princeton Review are probably the best known. In Canada, Oxford Seminars puts on courses throughout the country. Numerous private companies in each city or university in Canada put on courses as well. It is a good idea to visit the local law school to look at the bulletin boards where you will be sure to find advertisements for numerous LSAT prep courses. You can also find advertisements on other bulletin boards in undergraduate university buildings. It is helpful to ask around – ask classmates or friends that you know who have written the LSAT or taken a prep course to see what they think about the various prep courses offered in your area.

Oxford Seminars, LSAT Test Preparation Courses, Including Free Practice Prep Tests, Canada-wide, http://www.oxfordseminars.com/Pages/LSAT/lsat_about.htm.

Powerscore, http://www.powerscore.com/.

Kaplan, http://www.kaplan.com.

The Princeton Review, http://www.princetonreview.com/law/testprep/testprep.asp?TPRPAGE=5&TYPE=LSAT.

The LSAT Center, http://www.lsat-center.com/.

LSAC Prep Tests, https://os.lsac.org/Release/Shop/Shop_Books.aspx?po=Y#prep.

B. BOOKS

There are a number of books out there that are reasonable in cost and useful, but only if you are very self-motivated. All of these can be purchased from www.canadalawstudent.ca.

Kaplan LSAT 2005
by Education Center Kaplan CDN$ 20.30:
http://www.amazon.ca/exec/obidos/ASIN/0743251725/can adalawstud-20/701-3675836-3447539.

Kaplan LSAT 180, 2005 -2006
by Kaplan CDN$ 25.20:
http://www.amazon.ca/exec/obidos/ASIN/0743265297/can adalawstud-20/701-3675836-3447539.

Kaplan GMAT/GRE/LSAT 2004 Deluxe Edition
by Topics Entertainment. CDN$ 49.99:
http://www.amazon.ca/exec/obidos/ASIN/B00008QOE1/c anadalawstud-20/701-3675836-3447539.

Master the LSA T with Disk
by Jeff Kolby, Scott Thornburg CDN$ 25.64:
http://www.amazon.ca/exec/obidos/ASIN/1889057118/can adalawstud-20/701-3675836-3447539.

LSAT Logic Games Bible
by David M. Killoran CDN$ 38.50:
http://www.amazon.ca/exec/obidos/ASIN/097212960X/can adalawstud-20/701-3675836-3447539. One of the best selling books on Amazon.com.

Cracking the LSAT, 2006
by Princeton Review CDN$ 18.90:
http://www.amazon.ca/exec/obidos/ASIN/037576478X/can adalawstud-20/701-3675836-3447539.

Cracking the LSAT, 2005 Edition
by Princeton Review CDN$ 18.90:
http://www.amazon.ca/exec/obidos/ASIN/0375764119/can
adalawstud-20/701-3675836-3447539.

10 Actual, Official LSAT PrepTests
by Law School Admission Council CDN$ 46.87:
http://www.amazon.ca/exec/obidos/ASIN/0942639634/can
adalawstud-20/701-3675836-3447539.

The Next 10 Actual, Official LSAT PrepTests: Contains
PrepTests 29 -38
by Law Services Editorial CDN$ 46.87:
http://www.amazon.ca/exec/obidos/ASIN/0942639898/can
adalawstud-20/701-3675836-3447539.

10 More Actual Official LSA T PrepTests
by Law School Admission Council CDN$ 46.87:
http://www.amazon.ca/exec/obidos/ASIN/0942639804/can
adalawstud-20/701-3675836-3447539.

Ultimate Verbal and Vocabulary Builder for the SAT,
ACT, GRE, GMAT, and LSAT
by Lighthouse Review Inc CDN$ 14.67:
http://www.amazon.ca/exec/obidos/ASIN/0967759412/can
adalawstud-20/701-3675836-3447539.

The LSAT Advantage With Professor Dave 2004   -2005
by David Scalise CDN$ 34.20:
http://www.amazon.ca/exec/obidos/ASIN/0970175612/can
adalawstud-20/701-3675836-3447539.

LSAT For Dummies
by Amy Hackney Blackwell CDN$ 20.29:
http://www.amazon.ca/exec/obidos/ASIN/076457194X/can
adalawstud-20/701-3675836-3447539.

C. CD-Roms

I found a couple of excellent CD-ROMs at my local bookstore, which guided me through the various sections of the LSAT. I found these to be very useful, as they were interactive, inexpensive, and included a few prep tests. However, be aware that completing a test on a computer is not the same as writing an actual prep test on paper. You should be sure to try at least one, preferably more, prep tests in paper format, as you would in the LSAT exam.

Cambridge Educational Services,
http://www.cambridgeed.com/ooshop/controller.php?v=prd det&pid=185.

D. Strategies

There are many LSAT prep courses, books and CD-ROMs that may help you gain an edge over other LSAT test writers. However, everybody will find the best success through gaining a strategy of his or her own. This comes through practice, pondering and practicing again. Learn from your mistakes. Come up with short cuts and strategies that work for you. Increase your mental endurance through more regular, prolonged study sessions and repeated mock LSAT test writing situations.

Some people suggest that the score you receive on your first attempt at the LSAT is an accurate reflection of your potential and your abilities. I think that it is possible to increase your score, but you may need to work very hard and approach the LSAT in a new way in order to see a change in your score.

Other than that, I cannot really provide any strategies. You may find more helpful information in the books and CD-ROMs mentioned in this book.

E. TRY, TRY AGAIN!

Just don't give up trying to do
What you really want to do.
— Ella Fitzgerald

As I mentioned, I wrote the LSAT twice. This is common. It is an overwhelming experience the first time round, and many people are unprepared, especially in terms of the mental and physical strain and the endurance required. Alternatively, perhaps nerves got in the way. Do not be too embarrassed if you find that you need to write more than once. If you have decided that law is your dream, do not let this obstacle get in your way. Do not give up that easily. **Under normal circumstances, you can take the LSAT up to 3 times in any two-year period.** This applies even if you cancel your score or if it is not reported otherwise. You may hear from different authorities that LSAT scores do not differ greatly under normal circumstances from one test to another. You can find more detailed information on this at http://cachewww.lsac.org/pdfs/2004-2005/registration-book-ca-2004b.pdf (LSAT Registration & Information – Canadian Law School). This document includes a great matrix of differences between multiple test attempts. Do not be thrown off by this information. It is a matrix of averages. Not everyone will fall within his or her averages. If you feel that you might do better if better prepared, both mentally and physically, it is definitely worth trying the LSAT more than once.

F. DO NOT SHARE YOUR SCORE WITH ANYBODY!

What you think of yourself is much more
important than what others think of you.
— Seneca

As with your GPA, your LSAT score should be a private matter. Some students like to boast about their LSAT score. However, the LSAT is not always indicative of your real potential in Law School. There are so many other factors that come into play, such as ability to handle stress, social ability, study habits, whether some or numerous areas of law catch your fancy, your relationships with other law students and law professors, and so on.

Sharing your LSAT score is not necessary. It does not help anybody. It can make people feel bad about themselves, or cause them to categorize you. Unless someone shares their score with you in a non-hostile, non-threatening manner and in an atmosphere that you are comfortable with, I would suggest that you tuck your score sheet in a locked file cabinet and forget about it.

CHAPTER 3: THE APPLICATION PROCESS

*Law school has been described as a place for the accumulation
of learning. First-year students bring some in;
third-year students take none away. Hence it accumulates.*
— Unknown

A. WHICH SCHOOL?

There are quite a few law schools in Canada, and it can be difficult to choose which one is the best one for you. Assuming you have choices, you may want to consider some factors such as cost of living, moving yourself or your family, types of classes, size of faculty, and especially, where you would like to work after law school. Unlike in the U.S., students in Canada tend to stay in their home jurisdiction more often than not.

Law schools also tend to accept applicants within their province more readily. This is usually because they receive the most applications from within their particular province. Loyalty plays a role, and there is a hope that the law students will mostly stay within the province where they attend school. However, law schools readily accept applications from anywhere in the country, as well as international applicants.

There is some differentiation between law schools in the west compared to law schools in the east. It may seem obvious, for example, that Ontario law schools are primed to prepare students for Bay Street firms better than schools in Alberta or Saskatchewan. In turn, the University of Calgary and University of Alberta have more classes directed towards an energy-boosted economy, driven by oil and gas. Again, these are just single factors amongst many, and should not sway you one way or the other too readily. After reading this book, you may carry out further research into various law schools, the cities where they are located, and the types of firms and establishments within those cities. However, as you will see below, ranking various law schools is difficult and rather unscientific.

For some people, rankings of schools are the highest consideration because they want the best chance possible at a great job and a successful career.

a. Rankings – Do They Mean Anything?

Canadian Lawyer puts out a rank list of law schools in Canada each year, which is found at http://www.canadian lawyermag.com. I provide the rankings for the past few years for your convenience.

2000 Results:
1. University of Calgary
2. University of Toronto
3. University of Victoria
4. University of Moncton
5. University of New Brunswick
6. University of Western Ontario
7. McGill University
8. University of Alberta
9. University of Windsor
10. University of Montreal
11. Dalhousie University
12. University of Manitoba
13. York University (Osgoode Hall)
14. Queen's University
15. University of Saskatchewan
16. University of British Columbia
17. University of Ottawa

2001 Results:
1. University of Victoria
2. University of Alberta
3. University of Calgary
4. University of New Brunswick
5. University of Windsor
6. Queen's University
7. Dalhousie University
8. University of Toronto
9. University of Saskatchewan

10. University of British Columbia
11. University of Western Ontario
12. McGill University
13. University of Manitoba
14. University of Ottawa
15. Osgoode Hall (York University)

2002 Results:
1. University of Victoria
2. University of Calgary
3. University of Alberta
4. University of Windsor
5. University of New Brunswick
6. Dalhousie University
7. Queen's University
8. University of Toronto
9. University of British Columbia
10. University of Western Ontario
11. McGill University
12. University of Ottawa
13. York University (Osgoode Hall)

2003 Results:
1. University of Victoria
2. University of Alberta
3. University of Toronto
4. University of New Brunswick
5. University of Western Ontario
6. Queen's University

7. University of Windsor
8. University of Moncton
9. McGill University
10. University of Ottawa
11. University of Manitoba
12. York University (Osgoode Hall)
13. Dalhousie University
14. University of Montreal
15. University of British Columbia

2004 Results:

1. University of Calgary
2. Osgood Hall
3. University of Toronto
4. University of Victoria
5. McGill University
6. Dalhousie University
7. University of New Brunswick
8. University of Windsor
9. University of Western Ontario
10. University of Saskatchewan
11. University of Alberta
12. Queen's University
13. University of British Columbia
14. University of Ottawa
15. University of Manitoba

As you can see from the above lists, the rankings change from year to year. There are some inherent problems with the rankings put out by Canadian Lawyer Magazine. The first is that they are based on the input of graduating or recently graduated students. The magazine asks many questions about what the student thought of their particular school. It is in the student's best interest to score her school as high as possible, as a high rank supposedly ultimately looks good for that particular graduate. As well, the students polled do not really have anything with which to compare their experience. Most law students have only attended a single law school. Of course, one's own school is the best school.

If you just do a quick analysis on the rankings over the past five years, you will see that many of the schools jump from one end of the scale to the other. For example, Osgoode Hall (York University) was at the bottom of the scale at #15 (last) in 2001, #13 (last) 2002, then #13 (fourth from last in 2003). Then, in 2004, it miraculously moves up to the #2 spot. This example alone should give you a good idea of how much credence you should give to these rankings. Unless Osgoode received millions in funding, got a whole new set of faculty, and a brand new building, it is hard to justify a jump this big.

However, some things might be worth considering. For example, Victoria, Calgary, Toronto and Alberta are consistently at the top end, while British Columbia, Manitoba and Ottawa seem to be consistently near the bottom end. Again, digest this analysis with a grain of salt.

What would be more useful is a ranking as done by Maclean's Magazine[2] for the universities, which is put out each year. Many years ago, Maclean's did a ranking of the law schools, but for some reason they have not put one out for a long time. "To conduct the survey, Maclean's distributed a seven-page questionnaire to the country's 16 law schools and

---

[2] "Maclean's Law School Survey" *Maclean's* 6 October 1997 at 13.

mailed a second questionnaire to 3,997 law school graduates who had been called to the bar in the past three years. In all 1,227 – more than 30 percent – responded and their opinions kept UVic at or near the top of several categories."[3] Such a ranking would take into account the student / instructor ratios, research funding, job placement statistics, etc., and would be worth a lot more to a prospective law student or a prospective law employer.

Please do not put too much stock into law school rankings in Canada. They are not clearly indicative of the experience that you will have, or of the importance that a particular school will have on your employment chances. Law schools tend to be regional in terms of employment. Clearly, not all law firms hire exclusively from Toronto, Victoria, or Calgary. It would not make sense. It makes much more sense to hire locally as much as possible, as those candidates will show much more loyalty to the city and subsequently, the firm.

Be aware of those schools that consistently are at the bottom end of the ranking lists. Employers will perhaps consider more heavily the ranking of these schools compared to others. However, given the above arguments, this may be a cynical and superfluous approach.

Finally, I would add my opinion that an above average to excellent law student from any Canadian law school will have an excellent chance at career success compared to average and especially below average law students from those same schools. Do not fret about which school you will attend. Pick the one that is best for you, and then concentrate on getting yourself as high as possible in the grading curve. The rest will take care of itself.

You can find some good commentary on this topic at the following sites:

---

[3] http://ring.uvic.ca/97oct03/Top_ranking.html.

Margot E. Young , Faculty of Law University of Victoria, LL.B.s and Compact Disc Players: Accountability versus Marketability,
http://www.umanitoba.ca/faculties/law/LRI/Legal_education /young.htm.

Richard Moon, Faculty of Law, University of Windsor, Comment on Law School Surveys and Rankings,
http://www.umanitoba.ca/faculties/law/LRI/Legal_education /moon.htm.

Lisa Philipps, Osgoode Hall Law School, Comment on Law School Surveys and Rankings,
http://www.umanitoba.ca/faculties/law/LRI/Legal_education /phillips.htm.

René Côté, Departement des sciences juridiques, University du Quebec a Montreal, Comment on Law School Surveys and Rankings,
http://www.umanitoba.ca/faculties/law/LRI/Legal_education /COTE.htm.

Wesley Pue and Dawna Tong, Faculty of Law University of British Columbia, The Best and the Brightest? Canadian Law School Admissions,
http://www.umanitoba.ca/faculties/law/LRI/Legal_education /PueTong.htm.

b. Rising Tuition Costs!

When I started law school, I was prepared to pay about $5,000 per year for tuition and fees. I felt very lucky, as this number would be "grandfathered" for the next three years. In other words, I would not see an increase in the tuition that I paid from year to year, except for the usual university wide increases. However, the next incoming class would be charged a "differential fee" of about $2000, and the following class even more, so that tuition for them, including differential fees was $4000 more than I paid during the same year. It does not really seem fair, but the argument is made that this differential fee goes towards improving the faculty, and thus the opportunities and advantages for the law students. One or two law professors were hired during my second year, but other than that, I never did figure out what the differential fees were being used for. I was just happy that I did not have to pay so much!

The truth of the matter is that the cost of attending law school has skyrocketed in the past few years. Incoming students for 2004/2005 are looking at anywhere between $3,000 to $16,000 for tuition and fees, with an average across the board of approximately $9,454. Add to that amount the cost of living, gym fees, etc. and you are looking at a very hefty total for a year of law school.

It is not unheard of for a law student to amass a debt of $60,000 or more. Although salaries for lawyers do go up over time, especially compared to some undergraduate or graduate programs, prospective law students should be aware of the high cost and the potential debt-load that they may have to carry. It is a significant investment, and not one that should be taken lightly.

Fortunately, law schools are trying to increase the number of bursaries available to their students. One explanation for the differential fee was that those who are able to pay carry more of their own costs, allowing the school to assist those who are less able to pay. The fact that provinces are increasing the amounts of loans available to law students, as well as the increased amount of remission available to graduating students feeds the differential frenzy.

c. Considerations

As mentioned above, in making your law school choice, there are many considerations. You might want to contemplate class size, your family needs, proximity to friends, cost of living, course selection, job prospects in geographical area, reputation of the school's law review, reputation of some of the school's instructors, tuition, and many more things. Talk to family and friends about the factors that pull you one way or another. It may be helpful to draw a chart, assigning number values to various considerations, showing which are more or less important to you.

d. Should I Look South?

Many prospective law students consider the possibility of obtaining a legal education, and potentially legal employment in the U.S. There are some important factors to consider. The most obvious is tuition. Although tuition is rising dramatically in many Canadian law schools, most still do not touch the average tuition cost in the U.S. As well, unless you can afford, or can find some way to pay for, an upper rank law school, you may not find that you gain an advantage in obtaining employment, especially if you move back to Canada upon graduation. Tuition at a U.S. law school ranges from around US$4,600 per year at Brigham Young University (subsidized tuition for most of their students) to about US$23,000 at Columbia. For most law schools of stature, you are looking at upwards of US$15,000 per year.

Most U.S. law schools will consider an application from Canada. As well, all Canadian provinces will recognize a law degree from an ABA (American Bar Association) accredited law school – make sure that you apply to an ABA approved school if you are considering returning to Canada, or if you are planning to practice in most U.S. states.

If you are seriously considering practicing in the U.S., you should be aware that each state has its own unique entrance requirements to its own Bar. As of this writing, New York and Massachusetts accept an ABA approved Canadian law degree as "equivalent" to a U.S. law degree. California is another possibility for a Canadian law graduate, but realize that to be eligible to write the California Bar, you must first be called to the Bar of a Canadian province, or another American state such as New York. You will find the document at http://www.abanet.org/legaled/publications/compguide2003/ foreignlawschool.pdf very useful for this particular topic.

e. Special Status – Mature and Aboriginal Students

If this section does not apply to you, please read on. For those of you who think you may be included in these two demographics, please pay close attention. This information is key to you. It will also interest those who may have some misguidance or false information regarding mature or Aboriginal applicants.

There is a misconception held by many that Aboriginal students get a free ride in University, and subsequently in law school, and that they are somehow treated differently. There are rumours that Aboriginal applicants are guaranteed spots in law school if they apply, and that once accepted, they are graded differently. This is not true at all. I will try to shed some light on these preconceptions, while at the same time, providing information that will give Aboriginal applicants every advantage and opportunity to pursue a legal education.

The truth is that Aboriginal peoples are underrepresented in almost all areas of the Canadian economy. This underrepresentation is especially felt in law, an area where Aboriginal peoples require greater Aboriginal representation for all areas of law, including criminal, civil, and constitutional rights. More and more cases are coming forward and being heard in Canadian courts dealing with Aboriginal rights. Aboriginal peoples have unique rights entrenched in the Canadian constitution. As a result, there is a much higher need to have lawyers that are aware of, well versed in, and passionate about the rights of First Nations, Métis and Inuit. On the other hand, Aboriginal lawyers are needed to work for the Crown. Additionally, as more Aboriginal peoples are becoming involved in business ventures, there is a need for corporate and commercial lawyers who can be trusted and who have a good relationship with Aboriginal communities and individuals.

It is true that many law schools in Canada allot a certain percentage of spots available for Aboriginal and/or mature students. This percentage is often 10%. However, that does not mean that they always fill these spots or that the school is obligated to fill the spots with Aboriginal and/or mature students. The 10% number is a goal rather than a rule. As such, it is often the case that not all spots are filled by Aboriginal or mature students.

Some schools seem to attract a larger number of Aboriginal applicants. The College of Law at University of Saskatchewan and University of Victoria both have a relatively large contingency of Aboriginal law students. The University of Alberta does have an Indigenous Law Program, but the number of students was only 14 in 2004/2005 (out of a student body of about 500).

The process for applying to many law schools for Aboriginal students is a two-pronged approach. Aboriginal applicants have the option of attending a pre-law program at the University of Saskatchewan the summer before law school. Success at this program can lead to a conditional acceptance to some law schools. The program is aimed at preparing Aboriginal students for law school, in terms of study habits and curriculum. Attendees take property law. Successful students will get credit for this class, thus taking off some pressure during 1L. Acceptance is conditional on the student succeeding (in other words, passing) 1L. There are Aboriginal students who come out of the Saskatchewan program who do not succeed. However, the program supposedly does help many students to prepare and attempts to single out potential achievers amongst its attendees.

Aboriginal students can also be accepted unconditionally. This is often the case. This means that the Aboriginal applicant is rated alongside every other applicant. This happens before a conditional acceptance is considered.

Now, here is the truth of the matter. I believe that if you are an Aboriginal student (I was one), if you show sincere desire, and if you have a relatively decent GPA and LSAT score, then you stand a better chance than most applicants of obtaining acceptance to many law schools. Law schools that indicate that they encourage Aboriginal applications cannot say that they favour the idea of accepting an Aboriginal applicant. However, it is in their best interest to do so, as it looks very good for the law school when they can claim to have a decent contingency of Aboriginal students amongst their student body. However, remember this is the opinion of the author and that any reputable law school in Canada will never admit this idea. I just had to say it because I believe it to be true, and because I want to encourage any Aboriginal potential candidate to apply for law school because there really is a very high need for Aboriginal representation in law school and in the legal community.

For those of you who are not Aboriginal and who have read the above statements, please do not take a viewpoint that this is an unfair advantage given to Aboriginal students. The truth is that the number of applications from Aboriginal students is nowhere near what is needed to fill the 10% goal. It is also true that many Aboriginal people have faced extremely hard conditions in childhood and early adulthood, and that the odds are against them gaining access to university, let alone law school. I will leave the issue at that and hope that I do not create too much fuss.

If you are an Aboriginal applicant, I highly suggest that you do a lot of research on what each law school actually offers to its Aboriginal student body. Certain law schools claim to support their Aboriginal students in terms of counselling and study help. As much as you can, make sure that these claims are true. Also, do some research into what course offerings deal with Aboriginal legal issues. Most schools do not offer much in this way. However, in order to practice in this area, it is a very good idea to be as exposed to as much Aboriginal law as possible during your time in law school. The Kawaskhimon National Aboriginal Moot (see moot section of this book) is an opportunity that is open to almost every law student across Canada and is a great opportunity to learn what it is like to research and practice Aboriginal law.

Mature students are defined as those who are 35 years or older. As with Aboriginal applicants, there may be a certain percentage of spots "held" for mature applicants. As well, special consideration may be given to real-life experience. For example, if you have some connection to law in any way, you should emphasize this in your application résumé and statement of interest. Again, mature students are considered alongside all other applicants first. If they are not successful in this round, they may be considered in a mature student round. You should be sure to contact your law schools of interest to find out particular mature student criteria and standards.

A Word from the Wise – Practical Experience

If you really want to go to Law School, apply to multiple schools (I applied to 8). Apply the first day each school is accepting applications, and before you apply, connect with the head of the admissions committee at each school. Periodically check with the admissions coordinator at each school regarding your application. See if you can be placed on a wait list if you are not at first selected. Be persistent.

— Shawn Davis, University of Calgary LLB/MBA

Apply broadly. Do not have your sites set on only one school. Spend time on your application and letters. Proofread them. Have others proofread them. Communicate your intentions to your first choice school.

— Rob Nelson, Queen's University, University of Calgary transfer student

During my undergraduate degree, I was actively involved with my community through minor football and at school with the Students' Union. I think these extracurricular and volunteer activities definitely helped my application. As well, I worked really hard in my last two years of my undergrad to increase my GPA.

— Lorne Randa, University of Alberta

B. LL.B. vs. JD

Most Canadian law schools award the degree of LL.B. (Bachelor of Laws), while law schools in the U.S. offer the JD (Juris Doctor) degree. Toronto decided some time ago to offer a JD degree rather than an LL.B. They also increased their tuition dramatically, nearly on par with U.S. upper-end law schools. Ottawa has followed suit somewhat by offering a combined four-year LL.B/JD degree in conjunction with either the State University College of Law in East Lansing, Michigan or the American University (Washington College of Law) in Washington D.C. The JD is a U.S. degree, which enables the graduate to practice law in both Canada and the U.S. This seems to be a great idea, allowing for much flexibility for employment, and would be a great advantage to a prospective employer who does transaction work between Canadian and U.S. corporations. However, be aware that you will pay high tuition while attending Michigan or Washington for two years of the four-year program. The University of Detroit Mercy and the University of Windsor Ontario Schools of law were the first to collaborate to create a joint American/Canadian law degree program. Students complete 104 credits in three years and successful graduates receive both their JD and their LL.B. degrees.

Many other law schools have looked at the issue of the difference between the JD and the LL.B. There are many opinions on both sides; however, the predominant view at this time is that there is nothing wrong with the LL.B. in terms of gaining employment, especially within Canada. It is apparent that the combined JD (U.S.A.)/LL.B. would be an advantage if you wanted to work in the U.S. and could not gain exclusive acceptance at a U.S. law school, or if you think you might like to return to Canada one day. There is a long-standing tradition behind the LL.B. designation, and many people are not willing to exchange it for a JD designation easily. You can find some brief discussion of the matter at http://lssnew.law.uvic.ca/lss _phorum/read.php?f=12&i=1356&t=1351.

C. COMBINED PROGRAMS

It is becoming increasingly popular to combine a second undergraduate or a graduate degree with your law studies. This may be a very viable option for you. More Canadian law schools are offering a combined program, including:

LL.B./MBA [Business Administration] (Calgary, Alberta, UBC, Manitoba, McGill, Toronto, Victoria, Sherbrooke, New Brunswick, Moncton)

LL.B./MBA (M.P.A.) (Osgoode)

LL.B./MEDes [Environmental Design] (Calgary)

LL.B./MA in Asia Pacific Policy Studies (UBC),

B.C.L./LL.B./M.S.W. [Social Work] (McGill)

LL.B./M.E.S. [Environmental Studies] (Osgoode, Moncton), **LL.B./M.A.** (International Affairs) NPSIA Program (Carleton)

LL.B./National Program (Ottawa)
LL.B./National Program (Ottawa)

LL.B./MIR [Industrial Relations] (Queens), **LL.B./M.P.A.** [Public Administration] (Queens, Victoria, Moncton)

LL.B./B.Comm (Saskatchewan)

LL.B./B.A. (Saskatchewan) – 5 years

LL.B./B.Admin (Saskatchewan with U. of R.) – 6 years

LL.B./M.A.I.G. [Indigenous Governance] (Victoria),

LL.B./HBA (Western Ontario) – 6 years
LL.B./B.Esc [Engineering] (Western Ontario) – 6 years
LL.B./BSc [Science] (Western Ontario) – 6 years
LL.B./BA(History) [History] (Western Ontario) – 6 years
LL.B./BA(Kin) [Kineseology] (Western Ontario) – 6 years
LL.B./BA(Kin) [Kineseology] (Western Ontario) – 6 years
LL.B./MIT (Western Ontario)

Toronto offers a number of joint programs with their JD: JD/Certificate in Environmental Studies; Combined JD/Collaborative M.A. (International Relations); Combined JD/M.A. (Criminology); Combined JD/M.A. (Economics); Combined JD/M.A. (Russian and East European Studies); Combined JD/M.B.A.; Combined JD/M.I.St.; Combined JD/M.S.W.; Combined JD/Ph.D. (Economics); Combined JD/Ph.D. (Philosophy); Combined JD.Ph.D. (Political Science).

a. MBA/LL.B.

The LL.B./MBA joint program has become more popular in the last five years or so. The popularity of MBA's soared in the 1990's and an MBA became synonymous with success. The idea was that every great business leader had an MBA to back them up, and that it was impossible to make upper management without an MBA. Even successful businessmen and businesswomen took leaves of absences, or began part-time study to obtain an MBA for its status-symbol significance. Definite distinctions exist amongst MBA programs across the U.S. and Canada. However, because more and more people wanted to obtain MBA's, colleges and universities started accepting more students into their MBA programs, smaller schools started offering an MBA program, and soon the workplace became rather diluted with MBA's.

Despite the rise in numbers of people in Canada with MBA's, there are some important considerations. Extremely valuable information and skills can be acquired in an MBA program, such as how finance works and how to conduct yourself in business situations. However, obtaining an MBA is not easy, even today, and employers can look at this credential as proof that you have dedication and perseverance. The MBA is a challenging degree to obtain, with high workloads and, for many, very difficult examinations and assignments.

So, how do legal employers look at the MBA? It really depends. If you plan to work at a major national law firm, or at a firm that specializes in corporate and financial transactions, an MBA can be a genuine asset that may truly set you apart from your competition. An MBA can open up opportunities to be involved in files that you might not get to work on otherwise as a junior associate, unless you have knowledge and skills that duplicate what is learned in an MBA (such as accounting, financial or practical business experience). I have heard, although do not have anything to back it up, that a LL.B./MBA graduate can make more to begin with, but that salaries usually even out over a few years. More than anything, the MBA, along with your LL.B. will set you apart from your colleagues during recruitment time, will give you some social status within your firm, and likely with clients, and more important than anything, may provide unique opportunities to work with files that interest you, especially corporate and financial.

There seem to be widely differing experiences among those with a combined degree. I have heard from some who obtained this combined degree that they do not enjoy many opportunities to utilize the skills that they have learned in their MBA degree, and that those skills often go by the wayside. I have also heard that having the degree has done little for their salary. However, I know some individuals who claim to use their MBA every day in their legal work; anything from providing business information (lawyers cannot give business advice – only legal advice) to recognizing good business opportunities for themselves or for their firm.

One great advantage to the joint degree is the opportunity to have a backup plan in case you do not want to continue in law. For the extra year that it will take you to obtain the second degree, this may be good insurance for you as you ponder your career.

To be accepted into an LL.B./MBA joint program, you will have to gain acceptance into both the LL.B. program and the MBA program at your university of choice. Once you have accomplished this feat, you will make a formal application to the LL.B./MBA decision-making panel. I have heard that it is virtually guaranteed that you will be accepted to the joint degree program if you can successfully gain acceptance to both faculties within your university.

To apply for the MBA program, you will have to write the GMAT standard exam and apply directly to business schools where you are planning to attend law school. Make sure that you are fully aware of MBA application deadlines, GMAT exam timetables, etc. The GMAT is drastically different from the LSAT, and will require a very different approach in your preparation. The GMAT is scored using an adapting computer program that uses a unique point system. Basically, you gain more marks for answering early questions correctly. Getting those first few questions right can make a monumental difference to your end result. Make sure you are fully aware of this system, and come up with strategies to obtain as many points as quickly as possible at the beginning of the examination.

A Word from the Wise – Practical Experience

I am nearing completion of an LL.B./MBA program. I thought doing the combined degree would give me an extra arrow in my quiver. For any person with aspirations in business, I suggest you start off in the MBA program first year. ... Then at the end of the first year, if you decide that business is your niche, then you can opt out of the LL.B. portion and take only one extra year (or less) to complete the MBA. I would strongly consider that any prospective LL.B./MBA students do some reading on two simple financial principles: time value of money and compound interest. There is a definite opportunity cost to being locked into a joint program and a cost-benefit analysis is absolutely crucial.
— Shawn Davis, University of Calgary LLB/MBA

I considered the combined MBA/LL.B.. I thought that it would give me an added advantage in the market place. I decide against it for financial reasons. I could not afford another year of school.
— Rob Nelson, Queen's University, University of Calgary transfer student

b. B.C.L./LL.B.

Students in the undergraduate programme at McGill obtain both a civil law (B.C.L.) degree, which is used in Québec, and a common law (LL.B.) degree after completing 105 credits taken over three to four years.

You can take either the B.C.L. program or the LL.B. program at the University of Ottawa.

Victoria will potentially accept those students who have obtained a B.C.L. degree from another school into its school to obtain an LL.B. degree. These students will have to complete 3 semesters worth of classes to meet this requirement. There are other requirements that must be met. You can find full information at http://www.law.uvic.ca/Admissions/admission_LL.B.-bcl.php.

D. ACTUAL PROCESS OF APPLYING TO LAW SCHOOL

a. Admissions Information and FAQ's

Rather than go through each school's individual process, it is more prudent to provide links to the admissions sections of each law school's website, along with a link to the Frequently Asked Questions (FAQ) section, if available.

University of Alberta
http://www.law.ualberta.ca/students/prosp_adm_LL.B..htm#requirements
Apply online:
http://www.registrar.ualberta.ca/ro.cfm?id=211

Frequently Asked Questions:
http://www.law.ualberta.ca/students/prosp_adm_LL.B._faq.h
tm.

UBC
http://www.law.ubc.ca/prospective/guides.html
Admissions Guide:
http://www.law.ubc.ca/prospective/files/pdf/booklets/final_
LL.B..pdf.

U of C
http://www.law.ucalgary.ca/LL.B._Program/Admission.html
Frequently Asked Questions:
http://www.law.ucalgary.ca/LL.B._Program/faq.html.

Dalhousie
http://law.dal.ca/law_2466.html

Manitoba
http://www.umanitoba.ca/faculties/law/newsite/faq.php
Application Material:
http://www.umanitoba.ca/student/admissions/guide/pdf/law
/law_bulletin.pdf.

McGill
http://www.law.mcgill.ca/undergraduate/admission-en.htm
Frequently Asked Questions:
http://www.law.mcgill.ca/undergraduate/admission-en.htm.

Montreal
http://www.droit.umontreal.ca/169.htm.

New Brunswick
http://law.unb.ca/admreqfirst.html.

Osgoode
http://www.commonlaw.uottawa.ca/eng/admissions/how_to
_apply/index.htm.

Ottawa
http://www.osgoode.yorku.ca/reqhowtoapply.htm.

Queen's
http://www.queensu.ca/calendars/law/Admission.htm.

Saskatchewan
http://www.usask.ca/law/prospective/LL.B./requirements_a
pplication.php
Frequently Asked Questions:
http://www.usask.ca/law/prospective/LL.B./faq.php.

Toronto
http://www.law.utoronto.ca/prosp_stdn_content.asp?contentI
D=441&itemPath=3/6/15/0/0.

Victoria
http://www.law.uvic.ca/Admissions/about_admissions.php.

Western Ontario
http://www.law.uwo.ca/info-
prospective/admissions_first_year.html.

Windsor
http://cronus.uwindsor.ca/units/law/lawtop.nsf/982f0e5f06b
5c9a285256d6e006cff78/795e6935e3b3e76885256d870049b11
d!OpenDocument.

b. Strategies

Be sure to follow the instructions given in the admissions
and FAQ sections outlined above. Keep very close track of
deadlines both for applications and for submitted documents,
such as reference letters and transcripts. Also, make a note of
what the specific criteria are for each law school and whether
there are allowances made for mature or Aboriginal students.

Make sure that you send your application in on time and to the right person. If it is a rolling admission policy (kind of like first come, first serve), get your application in as early as possible. Make sure that you address your package correctly, and that you check and double check that you have included everything. Do spell checks on everything, and have someone else go over your application packages to look for errors. Submit everything on 20lb bond white paper. Nothing fancy. Do not give the admissions committee anything to set your application aside. Make it perfectly clean, concise and compelling.

Please see Appendix D for Sample Statements of Interest.

c. Résumé

The résumé is probably not really the most important aspect of your law school application. However, it is vitally important to include it, even if you are not requested to. This is because if it comes down to the wire between you and another candidate, a strong, well-written, and organized résumé could provide you with an advantage. It can be a convincing and accurate look into you and your potential. Take time to prepare a strong résumé.

Wherever possible, include any experiences related to law. Also, be sure to include all volunteer positions. This résumé is not really like a résumé for a job interview – it is a chance to really put yourself forward. As such, you do not need to be so meticulous about what to include. However, avoid an overly lengthy résumé. Keep it concise and keep it correct! No spelling errors, typos or formatting issues. Keep it on 20lb letter sized paper. No fancy stuff – just the basics.

d. References – What Kind are Best?

The best reference is a positive reference. Other than that motto, it can be a good idea to get a reference from somebody in the legal community. I got references from practicing lawyers whenever I could. Most schools will ask for a minimum number of academic references. You may also have to, or might want to, include a reference connected with community volunteer work.

Many people will be happy to work with you on the reference letter. You may want to provide a bullet list of things that you think are important to point out to the application committee. You might want to remind your referee of outstanding achievement in connection with the referee. Some referees will even be willing to slightly edit a pre-written reference letter. In any case, use tact and lots of respect when requesting reference letters.

Make sure that your referee is fully aware of the rules set out by each school. If the school requires the referee to mail the letter directly, provide the referee with a pre-addressed envelope with postage already affixed to the envelope. If the school requires a sealed envelope with a signature over the seal, make sure that this is done properly. You do not want one botched reference letter to mess up your chances. Let your referee know the potential consequences for going outside of the explicit rules.

If possible, get a copy of the reference letter. Put it in a file. The letter may come in handy later on. At some point in the future, for scholarships, summer jobs and even articles, an old referee can be called upon again to help out. You can provide a copy of the letter with your suggested modifications and ask the referee to print off another copy for these new purposes. It can save a lot of time and effort for both parties involved.

e. Deadlines, etc.

Please refer to Appendix B for all deadlines. Be sure to also consult the school calendar and website to ensure accuracy. Absolutely do not miss a deadline. There are no exceptions, and no excuse will be accepted. Do yourself a favour and get your application in on time.

Where applicable, you will want to be aware of the rolling admission rule, where a school accepts candidates on a rolling schedule, or as they receive their applications. Where this is the case, get your application in well ahead of the deadline.

f. Deferral

Many prospective students do not realize that there is often an opportunity to defer your studies for up to one year. Note that not all law schools offer this option. However, it may be a good option for you. Some examples of good reasons to defer law studies for a year are:

1. Finishing a graduate degree. I know of one classmate who attempted to finish a Master of Arts degree concurrently, without joint-degree status, and ended up spending both summers tackling the issue. Had he taken a year off before studying law, he might have circumvented the high stress he experienced. He also would have opened up his summers to potentially work in the legal field. Another student attempted the same with a Master of Science and ended up spending her first summer doing something that she did not feel would help directly with her law career. However, both of these individuals had made a commitment to finish their graduate degrees.

2. Getting an offer for a job that you just cannot refuse. I had a friend who received an offer to work for the federal government – something he had always wanted to do. He

managed to get a deferral from some of the schools that he had applied to and was able to try the government job. It was a great résumé booster, and a fantastic opportunity that he would have missed otherwise.

3. You need to save up for school. Now you can take up to a year to work full time, get prepared, and the pressure will be off, because you have already been accepted.

Be sure that you apply for deferral in plenty of time, and that you put forward a very strong case. Do not just assume that a school will hold a spot for you once you have received an offer. Also check into tuition fee hikes or differential fees that your faculty may have scheduled. If waiting an extra year will add thousands of dollars to your cost, you should consider this in your decision-making.

CHAPTER 4:
FIRST YEAR (1L)

Make crime pay. Become a Lawyer.
— Will Rogers

A. HOW TO HANDLE THE LOAD

a. Time Management

Managing your time during law school can prove to be very challenging. This is especially true during your first year (1L), when you can have up to seven courses to deal with. In my first semester, I had Contracts, Criminal, Constitutional, Torts, Property, Legal Research and Writing and Foundations to Law. All were full-year courses, except Foundations to Law, which was a half-year course. Most of these courses were 100% final exam courses, meaning that your final exam score, and nothing else, determines what grade you receive in that course. Legal Research and Writing included two written memos, a written factum, various assignments and a moot. In addition to coursework I juggled a slew of extracurricular activities, interviews for summer jobs, social activities, Canadian Bar Association activities, a part-time job, and family responsibilities.

For someone coming right out of his or her undergraduate degree, law school can be a huge jump in time commitment. It can also be a huge jump in personal autonomy, in terms of how you manage your time. Most classes do not have mandatory attendance and do not include scheduled assignments. However, some of your classes may include a participation portion in the evaluation breakdown. Many lecturers utilize the Socratic method, a method whereby the instructor may call upon you at any time to answer direct questions or postulate on a point of law. Lecturers usually expect students' active participation during class.

Depending on your professors, your school's philosophy of teaching and evaluation, and the way that your classes are structured over the three years, you may have a more or less challenging schedule. However, it is likely that your schedule will be much more challenging than your undergraduate studies regardless of the specifics.

To do really well in your classes, most of you will be required to prepare for each class each day. Preparation can vary between students. However, those who really excel seem to read all or almost all of their cases, prepare briefs for each case, and actively participate in class. This is a monumental task!

Assuming a schedule of six courses, consisting of three credit hours per week, and one consisting of two credit hours per week, you will be in class 20 hours per week. This may seem reasonable. You will not have any labs or tutorials in law school (at least there were none at my law school). You should, ideally, assume two hours of preparation time for each credit hour of class time. This is equivalent to 58 hours per week. You can break it down however you like. I knew many students who worked seven days a week. Some chose to take one day off. Some took two days off. It will depend on your stamina, and on the importance you place on personal time and other commitments.

This description may scare you. If it does, that is good. You should not embark on this challenge if you do not feel up to it. If you add up the numbers above, you are looking at an 80-hour school week, including preparation time and class time. If you have never done anything for 80 hours per week, this may not mean anything to you. If you have worked long hours at a job, you may have a better understanding. I will break it down for you. It is equivalent to 11.43 hours per day, 7 days a week. If you take a day off, you would be working for 13.33 hours per day, for 6 days. If you take two days off, it is 16 hours per day.

OK, I have scared you. You can't imagine spending 11 hours a day doing anything, let alone 16 hours a day, right?

Neither can most law students. The truth is that most law students do not spend this much time on their studies. There are a number of students who do, however, and I imagine that many of them are truly excelling in their studies and in their career. I cannot speak for these super-humans, as I consider them to be. I am well aware of their diligence, their commitment to their career, and their tenacity to beat everyone else.

Most law schools implement a very concrete grading curve, with rules about where professors and instructors must place students on the curve. What does a curve mean? It means that most students receive a grade of B, equivalent to a 6.0/9.0 or a 3.0/4.0. The important thing to realize about this curve is that it is a steep curve. The majority of students are right around the middle. A lesser number receive higher or lower grades. For most law schools, the grades look like this: A+, A, A- (for excellent work), B+, B, B- (for good work), C+, C, C- (for satisfactory work), D+ (for poor work), D (for a minimal pass) and F (for failing work).

You can see a good example of a bell curve at http:// academics.hamilton.edu/biology/smiller/curve.html. You may also find the commentary on grade inflation interesting.

I would like to provide some of my personal experience, not as a map for what you must do to succeed, but so that you can learn from my experience, and my mistakes. So, what did my schedule really look like? I can tell you that I did not spend 80 hours per week on law school. In my first year, I went to almost every class. I only missed class if I was sick, or had family obligations that had to be attended to. This means that I spent about 18-20 hours per week in class. I did most of my reading for most of my classes. This equated to about 50-60 pages some days. Other days only included about 20 pages of reading. So, I would average it out to about 40 pages per week. I was usually able to complete this task in about two hours per day, which I tried to fit in between classes, and after my children went to bed. It was not always easy to fit in during the week, so I tried to use Saturdays extensively to catch up. On top of this, I spent about an hour per class per week briefing and reviewing my class outline that I was building up over the term. This equated to a total of about 40-50 hours per week spent on schoolwork.

I did not do nearly as well as I should have in 1L. My 2L grades were far superior. What was the difference? Well, I spent some time over the summer preparing for my second year. I collected every CAN and outline that I could get a hold of. I collected every practice exam that I could get a hold of. And here's the kicker: If I was not learning something that would help me in writing the final exam while in class, I chose to pack up my stuff, go to the library, and do something that would help me on my final exam. As well, I chose to write as many papers as possible, as I felt there was a greater level of control over my final grade than with final exams. This is not true for everybody, but was true for me. Papers allowed me to manage my time over the semester. I could read only those things that I thought were important, and work on my paper research over an extended period. The actual writing process could then be completed within a week of time.

I learned a lot from my first year exam experience. I learned this: Do not get bogged down in facts. Do not get bogged down in analysis. Spend your time extracting the main arguments and reasoning of courts. Spend your time practicing application of legal principles to new sets of facts. How do you do this? Here is what I did: Before the class got rolling, I prepared my CAN as much as possible. I did this by extracting information from CANS or outlines that I had collected, from the commercial CAN, and where necessary, from Quicklaw™ or other summary sites that I found using Google®. I then spent considerable time reading over past exams – right at the beginning of the semester. This allowed me to become familiar with the types of issues that were important to look for during the course, and allowed my mind to ignore issues that had not been brought up on past exams. Just doing these two things saved me loads of time! I spent slightly less time on schoolwork in my second year. I chose only to read those cases that had been emphasized in class, or which had been confusing to me when we went over them. I spent a whole lot less energy in creating class notes, as I only had to fill in missing information as we went along in class.

You probably think that I show laziness through these techniques. You might be right. However, these techniques resulted in a lot more personal confidence going into exams, and resulted in superior grades going into that very important summer of articling interviews. My grades were so improved that recruiters simply ignored any faulty first year grades.

I also had a whole lot more fun! These techniques freed up tons of time to pursue other activities, such as my family, friends, leadership roles, business opportunities, volunteer opportunities, and more, all of which were also valuable in getting a job, as recruiters often like to see exploration of interests outside of the law classroom or law library. This is not the sole way to receive good marks in law school. There are many ways to go about it.

With any endeavour, time and talent play the largest role in success. For those of us with less natural talent, we must put in more time. This is the argument behind the LSAT – that those with natural problem solving abilities, and high analytical reasoning will excel in law school. Here is the thing: as I said before, most law students are right around the median. Most of us are average in relation to other law students. However, even those who are average are arguably in the upper ranks of society, in terms of intelligence, talent, diligence, and potential to earn an excellent income. So, unless you are on the upper end of those with Type A personalities (by the way, this personality type is extremely common in law school), why sweat it so much? I have numerous colleagues who have landed excellent jobs with slightly above-average grades.

The Dean's List in law school is sparse. Those people deserve tremendous respect, and many of them will probably go on to achieve great things down the road. It is my opinion that there are really only two ways to get on that list: time and inborn intelligence. Beyond time and talent, there is a third element that I think may help as well: having a parent that is a lawyer. There seems to be a high ratio of children of lawyers amongst Dean's List students. However, that is a personal theory.

So, to recap, there are many different ways to approach time management during law school. How you manage your time will depend on your personal goals, your inborn analytical talents, your recall ability, your interest in extracurricular activities or initiatives, your financial situation, etc. If you want to be at the top of your class, you should do your best to eliminate interfering activities as much as possible. If you want to be in the upper end of your class, make sure that you put in enough time reading, CANNING and practicing exam writing. Also, be sure to spend sufficient time building up your résumé in preparation for the upcoming job hunt.

A Word from the Wise – Practical Experience

Prioritize, develop a routine, and plan ahead. You will know long in advance how many papers you have to write, their

deadlines, and when your exams and midterms will be held. Look at your known commitments and make a plan. If you have two papers, a couple of midterms, and three exams, for example, you know you will not have anything due in the first month so why not write one of your papers? Similarly, if you have five exams, prepare as you go through the semester and aim to have your course summaries completed when classes end. That way you are only brushing up your knowledge between exams, not desperately trying to relearn something you never quite understood three months ago.
— Robin Penker, University of Alberta

Expect to be very busy. It is important to find balance; however, you may need to eliminate some less important activities from your life.
— Rob Nelson, Queen's University, University of Calgary transfer student

Work hard during the week by keeping up with your readings and reviewing your notes, but don't forget to enjoy life and take time for yourself during the week and weekends. For me, I also found that the busier I am the more organized I am. During down periods, when I didn't have much going on, I started to slack and ignore law school and studying.
— Lorne Randa, University of Alberta

Use CANS. Use a laptop in class to amend the CANS rather than printing them out and changing them after the fact. Stay away from people who like to gossip – you don't need your attention diverted.
— Shawn Davis, University of Calgary LLB/MBA

B. THE SOCIAL ASPECT – JR. HIGH AGAIN

In my experience, shared by many of my classmates, it felt like I was going back to junior high school all over again when

I began my first year of law school. I was assigned a locker, given a class schedule, told to line up for class materials and textbooks, and given a rather cheesy orientation, along with a class photo. All of my classes were in one building, there was a 'club day', and student union type elections for law school executive committees, complete with speeches and a vote. Small groups and cliques began to form immediately. Social activities such as softball day, a golf tournament and Friday Afternoon Beer Sessions [FABS] rounded out the first few months.

The atmosphere will be different at every law school, I am sure, but some things will make your arrival and survival a little easier.

First, **protect your stuff!** In a world with laptops and expensive textbooks, it is important that you keep track of your stuff. In my first year of law school there were over twenty laptops stolen from lockers and from the law library. You are in a school with many people, in some cases over 500 students. Add to that many other students who use the law library to study. I made it a point to keep my laptop with me at all times. This can be cumbersome and inconvenient at times, but worth it. Another good thing to do is to invest in a laptop lock so that you can lock your laptop to a table or some other secure item. This is especially useful if you have to step away to the washroom or to the water fountain. I had a friend who lost his laptop while checking emails on the library computer. He turned his head for a few brief moments, and whammo, his $1500 laptop was gone. That brings up another point. Back up your computer files constantly, daily if possible. That same friend lost all of his semester's notes because he did not backup his files. He had to scramble to get notes from friends, which put him at a great disadvantage.

Connect with positive, well-balanced people. It is my opinion that you do as well as the friends that you associate with. I found this to be true in secondary school. The same holds true for university, and especially for law school. The competition is fierce, the path can be lonely, and having positive, motivated, balanced friends can be an excellent source of energy and motivation. It can also be helpful when you need to confide worries, anxiety, or problems with somebody with whom you can relate to. Allies are incredibly important in law school. By aligning yourself with the right people, you can count on getting those missed notes that you need, sharing CANS or outlines, and finding necessary study partners when required. Further, having positive friends will make your law school experience a lot more fun. As well, when you finish law school, those friends will potentially become very important colleagues in the workplace.

Find your own space. It took me a while to learn this lesson. In preparation for my first year exams, I spent a lot of time at law school studying in the law library and seeking out people for assistance. This really hurt me in many ways. Firstly, classmates seeking empathy for their academic problems constantly distracted me. Secondly, the anxiety level was super-high in the weeks preceding exams. I felt tense all the time. The positivism that I needed was lacking, and I worried all the way through first year exams. Further, the anxiety carried into the summer months and really drained me. I would suggest either establishing a comfortable study space in your living quarters, or seek out another place away from the law school to study. I have successfully studied at the public library, where I did not encounter another law student, at another library on campus, and most successfully at a café. It is up to you, but find your own space. I would recommend using the space regularly during study time. It has been proven that having a regular space and time to study can increase your endurance and concentration ability. Make sure that you have access to or bring plenty of food and drink. Most libraries do not allow you to eat in them, but going outside for a quick snack is a healthy thing.

A Word from the Wise – Practical Experience

I was very conflicted. I didn't know if law was really for me; sometimes it seemed incredibly invigorating and other times it seemed highly mechanical and deathly dull. The first case I tried to read, I read three times, could not understand the obfuscatory language, and went to bed resigned to the realisation that not only would I be learning the law but also a new language. The case was only two pages long.
— Robin Penker, University of Alberta

I thought I had made a mistake and I was underqualified.
— Gayle Hiscocks, University of Calgary

I found the first month to be very overwhelming because of all the orientations and because reading cases and learning about law was a very new experience. It took me a while to get my bearings. I essentially had to find what worked for me in terms of studying. I was impressed by the different backgrounds of the other students.
— Kim Yee, University of Alberta

The first month of law school is quite overwhelming. I was not sure what to expect from the lessons and readings. There is a new language one learns in the beginning of law school, which at first seems confusing and hard to relate to. This definitely made lectures and readings hard to comprehend at first. I was also afraid of the Socratic style of teaching.

The amount of reading every night also seemed like a lot and also overwhelming, thinking "Will I have to read this much every night for the next three years?" I was also disappointed with the structure of what we were taught. The focus was mostly "this is what the law is and this is how one should look at things," while I thought law school would be more free thinking with room to explore options of what the law ought to be as well.

What impressed me was some of the great lecturers that I had during my first years (however, with that also came some really bad professors as well). I was also impressed with how open and accessible the professors were with students – most treated students like colleagues rather than students.

In terms of the atmosphere of law school, I found the social life of law school to be much like high school with cliques forming and some students' focus just being to party. I thought that law school would be much more of a focus on intellectual stimulation and challenges, but quickly found in the first month that this was not always the key focus. Being married, this aspect of school did not impress me.

— Lorne Randa, University of Alberta

C. FIRST YEAR SUBJECTS (SCHOOL BY SCHOOL)

Different law schools in Canada have adopted various core subjects for their law programs. You will not have any choice over the subjects that you study or what section you are placed into. You will not have any control over your class size, or which professor you have for any of your classes. This can be very frustrating and stress inducing. Nevertheless, it is just one of those pills that you have to swallow. The most important thing is to remember that you are in the same boat as the rest of your classmates, and that you are measured on a grading curve with the students in your section. Try to have patience with professors that rub you the wrong way. Look forward to 2L when you will have a lot more autonomy over your legal education.

Below is an outline of the first year programs at Canadian law schools. Most have a core of the basic areas of law, along with a legal research and writing course. This core will introduce the Canadian legal system, and will teach you how to read law cases, and to analyze legal situations, scenarios and problems. After 1L, you will have many options, but some schools still have required courses for 2L and 3L.

Law schools have shifted back and forth over time between more theoretical legal education and more practical legal education. There seems to be a recent shift towards practical legal education, which is a great thing in my opinion. It may be fun to learn about the history, reasoning, and theory of the law, but having practical skills builds confidence. Learning to scrutinize the law well is important, but learning to write a good contract, to negotiate, to advocate, and so on, is equally important.

Alberta
First year - Foundations to Law, Legal Research and Writing, Contracts, Torts, Criminal Law, Constitutional Law, Property Law
Upper years - Administrative Law, Company Law, Evidence, Jurisprudence or Legal History, Civil Procedure, Conflict of Laws, Professional Responsibility

UBC
First year – Contracts, Criminal Law & Procedure, Legal Institutions of Canadian Government, Legal Writing & Moot Court, Perspectives on Law, Real Property, Torts
Upper years – No Information Provided

Calgary
First year - Constitutional Law, Contracts, Legislation, Administration and Policy, Property, Legal Communication and Research, Torts, Crime: Law and Procedure
Upper years – second year – Civil Evidence and Procedure, Interviewing, Negotiation and Counselling, The Administrative Process; **third year** – Advanced Legal Research, Trial Evidence and Procedure, Trial Advocacy

Dalhousie
First year – Contracts & Judicial Rule-Making, Criminal Justice, Orientation to Law, Fundamentals of Public Law, Legal Research and Writing, Property in Historical Context, Tort Law and Damage Compensation
Upper years – **second year** – Civil Procedure, Constitutional Law; **third year** – The Legal Profession and Professional Responsibility

Manitoba
First year – Contracts, Criminal Law and Procedure, Constitutional Law, Torts and Compensation Systems, Property, Legal System, Legal Methods
Upper years – **second year** – Introduction to Advocacy, Evidence, Legal Negotiation: Skills and Strategies for Effective Representation, Civil Procedure, Corporations I, Administrative Law; **Either second or third year** – Trusts, Family Law, Introduction to Taxation

McGill
First year – Civil Law Property, Constitutional Law, Contractual Obligations, Extra-Contractual Obligations/Torts, Foundations of Canadian Law, Introductory Legal Research, Optional Complementary (Administrative Process, Criminal Law, Family Law, or Public International Law)
Upper years – **second year** – Advanced Civil Law Obligations, Advanced Common Law Obligations, Common Law Property, Legal Writing, Mooting and Advanced Legal Research; **One of your upper years** – Criminal Law, Judicial Institutions and Civil Procedure

New Brunswick
No information provided

Osgoode
First year – Civil Procedure, Constitutional Law, Contracts, Criminal Law, Property Law, Torts, Introduction to Canadian Public Law, Legal Research and Writing

Upper years – Completely optional courses
Ottawa
First year – Alternative Dispute Resolution (ADR), Constitutional Law (Canadian Charter of Rights & Freedom), Contracts, Criminal Law and Procedure, Public Law and Legislation (Statutory interpretation and structure of Canadian government), Property, Torts
Upper years – Civil Procedure, Constitutional Law II

Queen's
First year – Constitutional Law, Contracts, Criminal Law, Property, Public Law, Torts
Upper years – **second year** – Appellate Advocacy – Moots; **Any Year** – Civil Procedure course, a Substantial Term Paper, and a Practice Skills course

Saskatchewan
First year – Contracts, Criminal Law, Property I, Tort Law, Constitutional Law (Division of Powers), Constitutional Law (Charter of Rights and Freedoms), Legal Research and Writing
Upper years – No courses are mandatory

Toronto
No Information Provided

Victoria
First year – Constitutional Law, The Criminal Law Process, The Law, Legislation and Policy, The Legal Process, The Private Law Process, Legal Research and Writing
Upper years – Civil Procedure with Drafting, Evidence, one major paper

Western Ontario
First year – Constitutional Law, Contracts, Criminal Law, The Foundations of Criminal Law, Legal Ethics and Professionalism, Legal Research, Writing and Advocacy, Property, Torts

Upper years – **second year** – Administrative Law, Company Law, Evidence, Income Tax; **third year** – Civil Procedure, Trusts

Windsor
(LL.B program)
First year – Access to Justice – LL.B., Property, Contracts, Criminal Law and Procedure, Legal Writing and Research, Constitutional Law
Upper years – **second year** – Civil Procedure, Torts I
(JD/LL.B. program with Detroit Mercy)
Law I – Property Law, Contracts, Criminal Law, Constitutional Law, Access to Justice (JD), Applied Legal Theory and Analysis, Taxation
Law II – Civil Procedure, American Constitutional Law, Evidence, Torts I & II, Commercial Law – Sales, Law of the North American Free Trade Agreement (NAFTA), Comparative Civil Procedure
Law III – Payment Systems, Secured Transactions, Business Organizations, Canada U.S. Business Transactions

D. EXTRACURRICULAR ACTIVITIES

Law schools in Canada vary in terms of the number and types of extracurricular activities available to their students. I attended a law school that offered a myriad of opportunities. This section may not apply to all law students across Canada, but I feel I have something to say about this subject based on my own experience. Law school may be a lot like secondary school: opportunities can abound. Like a dessert buffet, it is tempting to want to try some of everything.

I joined Student Legal Services, both the Criminal Project and Civil Project. This entailed a weekly shift at the Student Legal Services house, along with work related to specific assigned files. I also ended up going to court, as a principal for some clients. The experience was great, although at times taxing. Remember, I did not know much about the law, and was handed a great amount of responsibility right away. Nothing like being thrown into the fire!

I also was an editor for the law school newspaper, first year rep for the Aboriginal Law Students' Association, Technical Director for the Faculty of Law Oratory Association, volunteer for a moot and volunteer for the Environmental Law Club. Retrospectively, this was far too much to expect from myself. However, in the competitive environment of law school, I believed that I needed to do everything possible to set myself apart in the upcoming summer job interviews. In addition, I was very interested in a number of areas of law, and wanted a taste of everything, as I had no idea what area of law interested me the most.

I would recommend getting involved, but minimize the involvement to a couple or a few activities that you are interested in and that will boost your résumé. Be aware of expectations for time and keep meetings to a minimum, and try to maintain a regular schedule for those activities. My *alma mater* has gotten to the point where there are just far too many student groups, and people are stretched beyond reason. I have also heard from many classmates, and recruiters, that it is important to show involvement outside of the faculty of law. Do not limit your extracurricular activities to your faculty, but do try to develop your legal skills and interests at a level that is comfortable to you.

Balancing work, school, extracurricular activities, and family was nearly impossible for me in 1L. I did not achieve my potential in terms of learning or grades and the stress that I felt was detrimental to all aspects of my life. My single biggest regret in law school was that I worked part-time during my first year. It allowed me to pay rent more easily, but retrospectively, I should have found another way to obtain the funds, such as with more loans. However, I should have limited my other extra-curricular activities before my part-time job. You know yourself the best. I only hold up a warning sign to you to monitor your time commitments carefully. More on this in a later section.

E. GRADES, GRADES, GRADES – OR, DOES IT MATTER?

Most of the literature that you will read about law school will tell you that grades are the single most important focus of your first and second years of law school. The competition is fierce for top jobs at law firms in Canada. Further, the competition is getting fiercer for jobs in general in Canada. I received better than average grades in law school, with improvement each subsequent year. I wish I had concentrated more on grades in my first year, but at the same time, I have little regret, and am well pleased with how things turned out.

Grades can be very, very important in 1L if you are vying for a summer job at a legal firm, which can subsequently lead to a guaranteed article at that firm. As well, stacking up your law school transcript before your second summer can be important in setting yourself apart to law firms. This is especially true in larger urban centres such as Toronto and Calgary. If it is your desire to work at a national or large city firm then make sure you put grades at the top of your priority list.

Although I believe grades are great indicia of commitment, hard work and intelligence, I do not think that they provide a complete portrait of the individual. This is why law recruitment committees also include such criteria as personality, experience, fit with the firm culture, and other personal definers in their recruitment material and information. Grades will definitely help you to get in the door of a law firm for an interview, but it is the interview that will ultimately determine your success in obtaining employment at a law firm. I am not aware of too many interviewers who would take an individual on the spot if they had a 4.0 GPA without interviewing them. Nor would they hire a 4.0 law student who made a terrible impression at an interview.

So, get your grades up as high as possible. This may be increasingly important as each year goes by, as article positions decrease, and as competition increases. However, do not ignore development of non-law related interests, skills, and personality. It is important to come across as unique, while at the same time convincing a recruiter that you will fit into their 'team'. This is a difficult thing to achieve, and I do not have specific advice for you to achieve the perfect balance. My advice is to work hard. Work harder than hard. Achieve your very best. At the same time, try to remain sane, fun, excited, and exciting. Bring passion to school every day, and bring passion to your interviews.

Grades are obviously more important at top law firms than they might be at smaller law firms. There seems to be a pecking order in the recruitment process. Top firms usually choose the top students. Many of those students end up choosing those top firms. However, it is not unheard of to have a very good law student choose a mid-size or small-size firm, or another legal setting altogether. I really admire those who choose for themselves, rather than going to where they are expected to go. Some high achievers are afraid that they will not be challenged or well compensated unless they are at top law firms. I have done research that challenges this notion.

One example includes Canada Justice, or a provincial justice office. These environments can be extremely challenging and rewarding, include a very decent and predictable salary, along with very good benefits. As well, the 'billable hours' are usually less demanding, which can lead to a much better balance. Another example is going solo in a small community. I am personally aware of such sole practitioner lawyers who bill $300,000 to $400,000 a year. Even after paying their business rent, expenses, and support staff salaries, they can make a very decent 6-figure income, often while working a very regular 9-5 type schedule. A third example is corporate counsel positions. Often, people who work as lawyers for corporations can earn very high salaries, be highly challenged, while enjoying very regular and decent schedules.

All of these examples require a lot of planning. They are not something that is necessarily achieved immediately upon graduating, or even soon after graduating. However, my point is that it is possible to be very happy as a lawyer outside of the big firms.

A Word from the Wise – Practical Experience

Grades in 1L and 2L are critically important because they are the grades firms see before summer and articling hires.
— Shawn Davis, University of Calgary LLB/MBA

I worked equally hard in all my years, although I did slow down a little in my last semester.
— Rob Nelson, Queen's University, University of Calgary transfer student

---

F. EXAM WRITING STRATEGIES

Law school classes do not teach you how to successfully write exams. The best thing that I ever did in terms of gaining an advantage in writing law school exams was to read the book *Getting to Maybe* by Richard Michael Fischl and Jeremy Paul. This book changed the way that I approached preparation for and writing of law school exams and is considered the pre-eminent resource on the topic of law school exam writing. I do not think that I could add much more to what these excellent authors outline on the subject.

You can find their book at http://www.amazon.ca /exec/obidos/ASIN/0890897603/canadalawstud-20/701-3675836-3447539 or on www.canadalawstudent.ca.

The only advice that I would add is to follow your instructor's or the testing supervisor's instructions very closely. As well, ask the instructor what colour pen they prefer, and if they prefer single or double spaces in the test booklet. Lastly, ask the instructor if they will give marks for an outline written by you in the test book. I have received marks in the past for points made in a quick outline written at the beginning of an answer to a question, even when I did not complete my full written out answer. Any extra marks that you can gain are worth scrounging for!

If you decide to attend review classes, prepare for them by doing practice tests first so you know what you do not know and then do not be embarrassed to ask questions.

G. LEGAL RESEARCH AND WRITING – STRATEGIES

Legal research and writing proved to be the most stressful and frustrating part of my first year in law school. Although I had a very competent instructor, this was a brand new way of thinking and of writing for me. If I could go back, I would have done a few things differently.

First, I would have asked my instructor, as well as other instructors for some copies of legal writing that was good. I would have asked for copies of "good" memos and "good" factums. As it was, I wrote these documents cold, without ever having seen an example of either. This would have helped me greatly to get into the mode of legal writing.

Second, I would have asked more help of the librarians in the law library. I was too proud to do this, and was afraid of bothering them. Once I hit upper years, I realized that that is what the law librarians are paid for. They will not give you the answer all the time, but they will do their darndest to point you in the right direction. This would have saved me hours and hours!

Lastly, I would have sought out more direct feedback, both from the instructor and from my classmates. This would have helped me to make improvements that were more cogent in my legal writing. It also would have helped me to make more convincing legal arguments based upon the law that I was researching. It is often hard to see through stacks and stacks of cases, but it is necessary, and it is a very good idea to learn this skill at the outset. In the case of 1L, the most difficult obstacle is not ignorance, but pride. It is hard to describe the pervasive fear of being discovered to be at the bottom of the heap. It is so real and so frightening that it becomes an impediment to asking for help, and thus learning.

You may find the following books helpful, although I have not reviewed them personally. They can all be found at www.canadalawstudent.ca.

Writing to Win: the Legal Writer
by Steven D. Stark CDN$ 17.47 - From a master teacher, a results-oriented approach to powerful legal writing that communicates, that persuades—and that wins.
http://www.amazon.ca/exec/obidos/ASIN/0385495927/can adalawstud-20/701-3675836-3447539

The Legal Writing Handbook: Analysis, Research, and Writing
by Laurel Currie Oates, Anne Enquist, Kelly Kunsch CDN$ 61.14.
http://www.amazon.ca/exec/obidos/ASIN/0735524874/can adalawstud-20/701-3675836-3447539

The practical guide to Canadian legal research
by Jacqueline R Castel CDN$ 53.80

http://www.amazon.ca/exec/obidos/ASIN/0459554301/can
adalawstud-20/701-3675836-3447539

You might also find this website helpful: Doing Legal
Rese arch in Canada
by Ted Tjaden – http://www.llrx.com/features/ca.htm.

In addition, this one: Best Guide to Canadian Legal
Research
by Catherine P. Best – http://legalresearch.org/.

H. SEEK OUT A REAL MENTOR

Some schools offer formal mentorship programs for first
year students. This may link up professors and law students,
practitioners and law students, or even lower-year and upper-
year law students. My experience with this was abysmal. It may
have been fantastic for other classmates or colleagues at other
law schools, but for me it was useless. The practitioner that I
was assigned to was extremely overworked, overstressed and
overcome with emotion about his own career. He signed up
for the mentorship program with very good intentions, I am
sure, but bit off much more than he could chew. As a result,
the time that I was able to squeeze out of him was
comparatively futile for both of us. Scheduled appointments
were postponed, invitations to attend court cancelled, and the
relationship quickly deteriorated and eventually disappeared by
my second semester of law school. I have heard similar stories
from classmates.

I would highly suggest seeking out a formal mentor of your
own choice and finding. A practitioner is great, if you can find
one. A family friend or colleague of someone that you know is
ideal, as they will feel more inclined to make good on their
commitment that they make to you, and may feel more
accountable for the relationship. Seek out someone who you

perceive to handle stress well, to be on top of their game, and most importantly, who shares some of your interests, both in and out of law school. Try to strike up a professional relationship, but do not be afraid to be friendly.

In my experience, a golf game or coffee with a chosen mentor is worth more than almost anything in law school. A small word of advice from a veteran of the law school and practical legal worlds can save you tons of time and stress, and can really help you in your goals to succeed. A good mentor can also be invaluable when it comes time to apply for a summer job or an article. A practitioner can be an excellent 'in' at the law firm that they work for, but also at other firms. Remember, they were once law students, and likely have maintained friendships with their past classmates or co-workers. The legal community is relatively small, and having an ally, or more than one ally, can be like gold when it comes to obtaining employment in your field of choice.

I. To work part time or not?

I worked part-time during my first year of law school. I did not get all of the scholarships and bursaries that I was hoping for, and so felt pressure to pay all of the bills that were trickling in within a few months of starting classes. I worked between 10 and 15 hours a week, which probably doesn't seem like much, but for me, it was the difference between feeling sane and running at the red line. It meant that I lost one day and evening per week for studying. Even though I only worked one day on the weekend, by the time I got home I was exhausted, and the last thing that I wanted to do was crack open the books to study.

I have known others who have been able to comfortably maintain a part-time job throughout law school. Most of those people really minimized extracurricular activities to accommodate working. Many people do not have a choice.

They do not receive sufficient scholarships or bursaries, or student loans, to cover their tuition, books, rent, food, and the rest. This is especially true today, as tuition costs have risen dramatically with deferential fees popping up all over the country.

If you can, I advise that you avoid part-time work during law school. If you do have to work, try to obtain flexible employment. Many people are able to maintain a research position for professors, which comes with a decent salary, and most importantly, flexible hours. However, be aware of your ability to avoid procrastination. It is easy to push work that does not have a deadline until tomorrow. The saying goes, "I have been thinking about writing a book on procrastination…but I never seem to get around to it." Try to get firm deadlines from the professor that you are working for.

J. THE BILLS ARE COMING – HOW DO I KEEP UP?

There are a few options to consider when your wallet starts getting too lean. The first is to obtain part-time work. Although it is not recommended, it is possible. I had a part-time job selling computer hardware and software in my first year of law school. I also had a part-time job as Editor-in-Chief of the Alberta Law Review in my third year. Lastly, I built web sites on the side during all three years, and this really helped to ease the financial burden of law school. I knew many students who had part-time jobs. It takes real discipline to pull it off, but it is possible.

The second option is to obtain a student line-of-credit. There are certain banks (Royal Bank being the favourite of professional students) who give preferential treatment to professional students, especially law and medical students. I was able to obtain a significant line-of-credit ($17,000) without a consignor. Many of my classmates met with the same success, often with even higher amounts. However, I warn you to be careful with this new financial power. Remember, you begin paying interest the day that you withdraw from a line-of-credit. One nice thing about a student line-of-credit is that you only need to pay the interest during your stay in school (revolving credit). However, be aware that this line-of-credit will convert to a loan upon graduation, and the bank will freeze the loan at the last amount of the loan. You will begin paying regular monthly payments, and your interest rate will increase. One word of advice is to withdraw the full amount of the line-of-credit before graduating. It is a very easy way to "qualify" without having to qualify. The line-of-credit will simply automatically convert to a loan, and will be amortized over a relatively long period. This is a good way to ensure that you have a little back-up cash during your first few months of articling, if necessary.

Third, check your school for supplementary bursaries or access fund bursaries. Depending on your situation, you may qualify for some assistance.

Fourth, appeal your student loan. If you have not obtained the maximum allowance from the government, you may be eligible for further loans. As well, if you reach the maximum allowance, you may be eligible for certain bursaries and grants, such as the Millennium Bursary or Canada Study Grant. Further, you may qualify for remission on your loan upon graduation. I maxed out my student loans each year, and as a result, was credited $16,000.00 towards my National Student Loan upon graduation. However, be sure that you maintain a strict budget and avoid the temptation to go and spend all of your loan money prematurely. It will bite you back when you graduate.

Fifth, live off credit cards, family help, and whatever other legal sources you can think of. Put your energy into your studies and put yourself in a position to win scholarships and/or bursaries from your faculty and university. Most schools have an abundance of these, and you may be better off staying away from part-time work to give yourself a better chance at winning one or more of these. I often wish I had avoided working part-time in my first year, as I believe my GPA would have been higher and I would have made a lot more from scholarships and bursaries.

A Word from the Wise – Practical Experience

I paid for law school from personal savings, a small contribution from my parents, financial support from my wife (i.e. living expenses), part-time and summer work during the year, and a large part from scholarships - particularly in my last two years.
— Lorne Randa, University of Alberta

K. AVOID LAW SCHOOL TUNNEL VISION

Law school can be overwhelming for some people. It is easy to be consumed by the intensity of your coursework, moots, exams, job applications, etc. It is easy to get overzealous in your extracurricular activities in an attempt to beef up your résumé. You may feel an overactive desire to make contacts in the legal field. All of this can lead you to feel that you must attend every activity, every meeting, every open house, and every social event announced. I was overcome with a desire to do everything and be everything related to law school, and it was not until about midway through my second year that I realized that I was trying to do too much. I also came to realize that recruiters were not going to expect me to be superman, involved in every activity or opportunity under the sun. In speaking to some various mentors in the legal field, I came to realize how important it is to have some variety in your life, meaning to have a life outside of law school. This was a major revelation for me, and I quickly adopted this mentality.

Recruiters will be interested in various activities that you are involved with in the legal field. However, they will also be very interested in non-legal activities that you spend your time on. For example, are you involved in sports? Sports involvement can mean that you are a team player, or that you have a certain drive or ambition that will be important in your legal career. Are you involved in your community? Will you be willing to reach out to the community and offer pro-bono work? Do you have connections or potential connections in the community? Are you doing yoga, or taking a quilting course? These types of activities can be indicators that you seek to control stress, and attempt to have balance in your life. Are you involved in entrepreneurial activities? This type of activity can indicate a certain drive and self-motivation. You do not have to do all these, but choose something that suits your personal needs and interests. Whatever it is that you get involved in outside of law school can set you apart amongst a very large pool of competition. It can also provide opportunities to connect with a recruiter. Perhaps you share a similar interest, or perhaps you are involved in something that a recruiter has always been interested in and would like to know more about. Sometimes you receive an invitation to an interview because you seem interesting to the job or articling committee and they want to meet someone who does such and such.

To recapitulate, do not feel that you must focus all your energies on law school and law-related activities. I have known classmates who have been involved in amateur sport at a high level, active in the political community, involved in their children's school or sporting activity, volunteers at geriatric units, volunteers for advocacy groups, and many other things during law school.

Looking outside of the walls of your law school can also provide an outlet for you, or an opportunity to just give it a rest. Your mind is constantly working out legal problems, trying to remember important principles from various cases. Your mind will appreciate the opportunity to actively forget about these things, even if only for a while each day or each week.

You will find that it is important to achieve balance once you enter the practical field of law. Working on this aspect of your life in law school will lead you to have good habits and aspirations once you are working as a lawyer.

L. 1L ATTITUDE AND BEHAVIOUR TIPS:

> *I got a simple rule about everybody.*
> *If you don't treat me right – shame on you!*
> — Louis Armstrong

a. In Class Comments

One of the things that shocked me about law school was the Socratic method of teaching employed by many law professors. You have to be on your toes all the time in those classes that employ this type of education. It can be stressful if you are not prepared.

This type of teaching style does not work for everyone. Some people buckle under the pressure. Some lose their cool and get lost. Unfortunately, professors often pick on this type of student. One of the things that bothered me most in law school was students who could not keep their thoughts to themselves in such situations. If a classmate is struggling in this type of stressful situation, the last thing that they want to hear is snickering behind them, or a whispered comment about them. Keep your thoughts to yourself. Who knows when you will be in the same situation where you do not have the appropriate answer? Alternatively, perhaps you will have had a bad night the night before, and been unable to fully prepare for class. Keep that in mind before making comments. Law students are supposed to help each other through the grind, not grind each other down. Do unto others ... remember the Golden Rule.

On the same note, it is important to be humble in a law classroom. It does not take long to identify the student that just will not shut up or the one who cannot help but to provide a full and unannotated answer to a professor's rhetorical question. This type of behaviour does nothing but irritate classmates who are there to learn about the law from the professor.

If you have something useful to say, or rather if you have a question that you think will be of use to the entire class, feel free to share with the class and with the professor in a succinct, professional manner. If you feel that you want to have further discussion about the subject matter at hand, arrange a meeting with the professor. If the professor thinks that he should share something about your discussion with the rest of the class, he will usually bring it up in a subsequent scheduled class.

Do not come across as a know-it-all. You may know the subject matter inside and out. You may feel a need to prove this to the professor and to the rest of the class. You are well advised to save your genius for the exam. You will keep more friends this way, and will make life a lot easier on yourself.

b. Sense of Humour

> *Congratulations, you have a sense of humor.*
> *And to those who didn't: Go stick your head in the mud.*
> — Jesse Ventura

Law school can be a very serious place. With the high levels of competition, the ceaseless discussion of articles, summer jobs, grades, and exams, it can become a rather depressing place for some people. That is why it is important to remain calm and have a sense of humour about things. Remember to sit back occasionally and look around you. You are all in the same boat together. Most people succeed. Very few people die from law school.

Laugh about the way that your law professors conduct themselves using silly nineteenth century mannerisms. Take joy in the junior high school antics that go on around you. Marvel at how seriously people take themselves. For example, I had one fellow two years behind me who wore a suit to school every single day of his first year of law school. He might have been trying to make an impression, or trying to keep himself serious, but, in my opinion, it ended up doing him more social harm than good. Do not sweat things too much. You have succeeded in making it to law school, and that in itself is something to celebrate each day that you are at law school. You are really among the elite. Tell yourself that you belong, and that you have the intellectual, emotional and physical tools to battle with the best of them.

Ask yourself often, "What is the worst that can happen?" It is relatively difficult to fail out of law school. Further, no one has ever died from failing in law school, that I know of. The worst that can happen is that you might have to challenge a particular exam, and then rewrite it, or have to do a year over again. I have one colleague that did this and succeeded the following year. The most horrible thing that could happen is that you may have to choose another career, and there are probably more reasons for this alternative than simply failing your exams.

Be sure to celebrate your victories. A victory can be finishing your first year moot, getting through midterms or final exams or completing that first year memo. Celebrate every step of the way, and you will be a lot happier. I found it helpful to give myself rewards, even for the small stuff. For example, if I could read for an hour straight from a law textbook, I would treat myself to a cup of tea or a hot chocolate. The next time, I got the reward if I could sustain two hours. Law school, like any big challenge, is a series of little baby steps. Build upon your successes and soon you will reach the finish line.

A Word from the Wise – Practical Experience

The first assignment is always stressful. Nobody really knows what is going on and how much work to do. Inevitably, people stress too much and work too hard on the first memo.
— Rob Nelson, Queen's University, University of Calgary transfer student

With the memo, I tried to brainstorm all the possible issues that might be involved in the fact scenario given. I then researched those issues extensively in textbooks, Quicklaw™, the Canadian Encyclopaedia Digest (CED) and Canadian Abridgement. I also spoke with classmates about the topic to see if I had missed any issues or key cases. With all this info obtained, I then pulled out the relevant cases needed and wrote the memo following the outline provided to us as close as possible. Lastly, I edited my memo several times to make sure it was logical, coherent and cohesive.
— Lorne Randa, University of Alberta

c. Share Your Notes!

There is nothing worse than beginning your exam preparation and finding that you have gaps in your class notes. Perhaps you were sick one day – it happens to even the best of us – or you were caught up in a meeting, or you just plain did not feel like going to class. Losing a class worth of notes can be devastating, depending on the professor or the class. The only viable way to fill these gaps is to get notes from someone else. The most viable way to get those notes is to freely share your notes with others at every possible opportunity.

What is unique about law school, compared to most undergraduate programs, is that exams are not, for the most part, testing your ability to memorize facts, figures, numbers, or events. They are testing your ability to read a situation, analyze it and come to a logical conclusion that is compatible with the law. As such, even if you have the very best notes in your class, it won't really do your classmate that much good if they haven't been able to connect the dots while they are in class and while they are studying. In other words, sharing your notes is not going to put you at a great disadvantage when it comes to exam time. Chances are that you will have grasped the knowledge better than your classmate that missed the class anyway, and that you will better be able to recall things from your notes than they will be able to. On the flip side, if you have gained a reputation for not sharing notes, you will not likely be able to fill the gaps when faced with an emergency that causes you to miss a class.

In short, work with the system, rather than trying to hoard information. It will pay off in the end.

d. Don't Share Grades – Period

With the exception of your Mom, Dad, husband or wife and maybe your best friend (that isn't in law school), do not share your grades with anyone. It does not help anybody, including you. It leads to negative emotions, either on your part, or on the part of your confidant. It leads to unnecessary gossip, unnecessary stress and ultimately does more harm than good most of the time. Assume that everyone else is getting great grades, and work hard to keep up with the rest of the class. Remember, everything is graded on a curve (the most common grade is a B), and that your goal is to stay on the right side of that curve. Also, remember that it is more important to show improvement, dedication and perseverance when it comes to recruiters. True, some recruiters will have a bias towards those who receive top marks. However, do not count yourself out if you have received some low marks in your first year. Recruiters look at a lot more things than grades, contrary to popular opinion. More on that later.

e. Keep Your Opinions to Yourself

I mentioned that it is important to keep comments to yourself during class time. It is equally important to keep negative thoughts, opinions or gossip to yourself while at law school generally. Because law school is inherently competitive, stressful, and often full of pessimism, do your best to curb those trends. You will be much happier in the end, as will your classmates. Keep opinions about professors, exams, deans, classmates and such to yourself. Everybody already knows if a professor sucks. They already know if a classmate is irritating. These things do not really need to be pointed out. If you have a problem with an individual, confront them individually, not through a group.

M. 1L MOOT

The first year moot, which is a required element of most Canadian law schools, can be the most rewarding experience or the most regrettable and terrible experience of your law school career. Classmates of mine have been brilliant in their moot, and others have absolutely bombed. There are many urban myths that fly around about the first year moot. Don't be surprised if you hear of former mooters fainting during their moot, swearing at the judge panel, of going absolutely blank, of being forced into submission by a overbearing moot judge, of even peeing themselves during their moot. No doubt about it, the moot is a challenging and, for many, intimidating experience.

The solace comes in the fact that almost nobody, if anybody, fails his or her first (or second) year moot. Along with the urban legends listed above, you will hear about how that same person that fainted still passed their first year moot. The moot is a pass/fail portion, usually combined with the legal research and writing or constitutional class in your first year.

Along with the moot, you will likely be required to write a formal factum, which you will submit before the moot. You will be marked on this document, so treat it very seriously. Check out www.canadalawstudent.ca for an example of a factum.

For your moot, you will be paired up with somebody, so be prepared to drop any pride or selfishness. It truly is a team-effort, as you will write your factum with your partner(s) and will present alongside them. The moot is meant to simulate court proceeding in every way possible. You will submit your formal factum, dress up in formal robes, sit in your proper place within the simulated court room, and will follow all formal court procedures throughout the moot.

Teams will be separated into the Appellant, the Respondent, or the Defendant and the Prosecution, depending on the case at hand. You may also have the opportunity to represent an Intervener, which is a party that has an interest in the case at hand, but is not a direct party to the action. The Intervener is more like an advocate of a particular cause. The Intervener will also be responsible for submitting a formal factum, and will have an opportunity to address the court. This address will also be formal, and according to the rules of the court.

a. Strategies to Prepare for the Moot

Once you have written your written factum (your researched and written concise submissions) in preparation for the moot, which is the usual protocol, most of your work will be done in preparation for the moot. By now, you have worked extensively with the given case, and you probably know a lot more about it than you realize. There are some things to be aware of as you prepare for your oral presentation or moot. There is no way to fully prepare for the questions that the judges may pose to you. Each of the four students (or more if there are interveners involved) will have their own opportunity to address the court. Your presentation should be in line with your co-counsel, and should avoid overlapping issues; however, the judges can ask you about any matter that you may be representing on your side.

Your presentation will have a time limit, and a timekeeper will probably keep very strict track of the time. Your presentation will include time to introduce your position along with opportunity to answer questions posed to you by the judges. Depending on the judges that you get, you may spend most of your time presenting, as with a speech, or you may spend all of your time answering questions. It is not unheard of for judges to jump in with questions before you can get two sentences out. Some students are very intimidated by this prospect. However, in my experience with mooting, this should be a welcome opportunity to show what you know. It is hard to feel that you have caught the attention of the judges if they just passively listen to you.

Given the information outlined above, it is best to prepare for anything that may come your way. You should prepare an introduction, which you should memorize as much as possible to avoid reading a prepared speech. Many students prepare an outline with as little detail as possible, to avoid reading straight from their paper. Other students have found index cards to be very valuable for outlining their ideas. The key point is that judges are not impressed (nor are instructors) by verbatim reading. All of the judges and your instructor will have read your written factum and will be aware of the arguments that you have presented in your factum. The oral presentation is an opportunity to put forward fresh ideas, or to clarify what you have said in the written submissions. It is also an opportunity to showcase your personality. Now is your chance to live out your litigation dreams (or nightmares).

Focus on the law, not on performance. Do not sweat it too much. You will make it through your first moot. The advice in this section of the book is provided in hopes that you will be able to cope with the stress of the moot more easily. It is not meant as a formula for success or rather a formula to avoid failure. Failure, in my opinion, is not really an option because it is not possible.

You may decide that you never want to get involved in mooting or litigation after your first moot. Alternatively, as with myself, you may find it exciting. Many people decide their career direction as a result of their first moot. Take it as an opportunity to learn about yourself and your potential.

I do suggest that you practice your moot. Practice with your co-counsel partner, practice with your girlfriend or boyfriend or spouse or brother or sister. Practice in front of the mirror. Practice in front of your "competition." Practice in front of practice judges, whom are often available – usually upper year students who can give very valuable advice.

I would avoid talking to too many upper year students about their experience, as this can do more harm than good, especially if they tell horror stories. Save the war stories for after the fact. Keep your focus on understanding your case, your position, and potential hang-ups. One last piece of advice – before you go into your moot, write a list of as many possible questions that might be asked about your case or your position and practice answering them. Practice this repeatedly, and you should not fail. I mean, you will not fail.

A Word from the Wise – Practical Experience

The main thing I did to prepare for the first year moot was to talk to different students in upper years. I found that they were much more helpful in the practical hints than my instructor was in the course.

— Jamie Johnson, University of Alberta

For my first year moot, I reviewed my team's factum many times to get a strong understanding of all of our arguments and cases. I also made sure that I understood our opponent's case and possible arguments they may make towards my position. I then wrote out a very structured and logical speech. This speech I practiced in the car, in front of a mirror and in front of my wife in order to be comfortable speaking about the issues and arguments. I practiced my arguments in front of my partner who would challenge me with questions related to my case.

— Lorne Randa, University of Alberta

b. How to Compose Yourself

First, get to the moot location in plenty of time. Make sure to bring your factum (tabbed with any helpful notes in margins or on sticky papers), your presentation outline, including your main points or arguments, and perhaps some concise notes to help you answer potential questions. Once you have gowned, make sure that your notes are in order and easily accessible, and then sit back, take some deep breaths and relax. Wait patiently for your turn. If you are not first, then take the opportunity to listen to the others and the questions posed by the judges. If helpful, make some notes to yourself in your materials based on the previous presentations and questions posed. You may also find it useful to make note of any important answers given if they are pertinent to what you want to say.

To the best of your abilities, stick to the rules of etiquette, which you will hopefully learn from your instructor. Address your classmates as your friend. Address the judges in the appropriate manner, as taught to you by your instructor. Avoid personal opinions and frame all arguments or comments as a submission on the part of your party (i.e. "I submit" or "I respectfully submit" or "we submit" or "we respectfully submit", etc.).

Listen very carefully to questions posed by the judges. If necessary, ask the judge to repeat the question (however, avoid doing this too often, as the judge can get irritated or think that you are stalling). If necessary, paraphrase the question for clarification. Also, do not be afraid to take a moment or two to collect your thoughts or to flip to the appropriate spot in your notes. If you require more time than this, ask the judges to give you a few moments. Once you have calmed your nerves, or thought of a smashing response, dive in. If you have done your homework, you will be able to come up with some answer in almost every instance. If you cannot, then find something to say. Avoid going too far down a road if you think it feels dangerous. Moreover, if you feel that you just have nothing to say, admit it and move on. A good response for this may be, "I do not readily have information on that particular issue or matter and would have to take the matter back to my office for consideration before answering your question. May we move on to another question or matter?" Try to stay composed. Do not let the judges fluster you, although they may test you. Usually where people are hung up is when they keep being attacked by a judge on a particular matter. Stake your position, and do not flinch. It is better for you to admit that you cannot answer a question and move on than to be caught floundering.

Show as much respect for each of the participants, especially the judges, and you will make it through your 10 or 15 minutes without too many hitches.

c. The Debrief

Good moot coordinators will provide an opportunity for feedback to the mooters from the judges. This can be very intimidating, especially the first time. For the most part, you will receive positive feedback. However, be prepared for some criticism. You may be critiqued on the content of your arguments, but more comments will centre on your presentation style, your ability to address questions, and your general impression made upon the judges. Your instructor will be the one critiquing your arguments, so do not sweat the judges remarks too much. Your written factum will carry far more weight in most instructors' eyes than the oral presentation. The moot is simply an opportunity to practice oral advocacy skills, to introduce you to the world of litigation, and to give you a taste of what may come in subsequent moot opportunities in your upper years.

Be sure to try to get a debriefing session with your instructor if possible, or if desirable. The moot is a great opportunity to grow personally, and any feedback that you can get will help you to gain a position on upper year moot teams, and hopefully to excel at competition.

As well, try to get together with your moot partners and/or opponents to discuss what you could have done better. Be sure to provide constructive criticism that will truly help your colleagues become better mooters and litigators. Do not harp on personal style issues. Focus on how arguments could have been stronger, how a point could have been better made, and how to better handle questions. You should expect the same, so do not feel that you have to sit and listen to someone banter about your personal style. Ask for courtesy if necessary.

N. Finding a Summer Job

The race for a summer job begins on day one of law school (if you want to ride on that track). Find out if you want to ride on that track later in this section.

What do I mean by "the race begins on day one"? I have indicated previously that law school is a very competitive place. I am going to repeat this fact with some emphasis here. The number of summer jobs available at law firms to first year law students are very few. This is especially true in some cities where law firms tend to hire second year summer students over first year summer students. Read this portion of the book carefully – it can be rather complex.

In some cities, law firms are anxious to identify potential articling candidates as soon as they can. They are also anxious to find students that will be loyal to their firm, and equally as important, to the city where the firm is located. This is true for some of the less-major cities, such as Edmonton and Regina. Summer employment allows firms a great opportunity to 'interview' an articling candidate for four whole months. It also allows them to get some of the less-attractive tasks done at a relatively low wage.

However, summer jobs are not about the summer alone. They are about recruitment for the all-important article. Normally, firms cannot recruit or offer a student an articling position except for during a specific period during the second summer of the student. These dates are set in stone in the various jurisdictions, and there is no deviance from these rules without consequences. The rules are there for both the firms and for the students' well-being and fairness. I will speak about these rules in the articling section of this book. However, a firm can get around the usual articling rules about recruitment through the summer job program. A firm can offer a summer student an articling position at the end of the summer employment.

So, a classmate can gain a great advantage early on in their law school career by landing a summer job as soon as possible. By doing so, they will potentially avoid the article competition later on, and can rest easy during their second and third years. It may sound preposterous, but a student can potentially have their career laid out before them as early as January of their first year. Perhaps you can see why I said that the race begins on day one.

If this route sounds attractive to you, there are some things that you will have to keep in mind, right off of the start line:

Get to Know the Different Firms. For summer positions, do they hire first year or second year students generally? How many summer positions do they offer? Do they normally offer articling positions to their summer students at the end of the summer term? Are you interested in the firm? If they ask you to eventually article with them, is that a decision that you would be comfortable in making?

Attend Open Houses Held by Firms. Many firms will make visits to your law school to get to know potential candidates. This can act as a pre-screen interview process, so take it very seriously. Although you may be a face in a rather large crowd, if you are able to make even a slightly positive impression at this type of function, it may be that the recruiter will remember you at interview time. Make sure that you dress well for these functions. They are usually formal, so here is an early chance to break in that new suit that you bought before law school. Do not show up in khakis, jeans, or other informal wear. The general rule is to overdress. Nobody will ever think badly of you in this situation if you dress better than the rest of the crowd.

Make as Many Contacts as Possible in Law Firms. You may be able to make contacts through your assigned, found or chosen mentor, friends, professors, and your career officer. It does not matter, as long as you can make some contacts. You will utilize these contacts in both your résumé and your interview (discussed below).

Be very aware of application deadlines and interview times. The application process will vary from school to school, and from city to city. Know the dates as early on as possible, and make note of them.

Get Your Résumé and Cover Letter in Order Quickly. You will want to update your résumé as soon as possible. Do not leave this until the last minute. You will be very busy with classes and exams to take care of this stuff when it counts. You can always add to these documents at the last minute.

Get Feedback on Your Résumé and Cover Letter. This is a tricky one because you may not want to show it to classmates who will be competing with you for the same positions. Look to career officers, contacts who are already lawyers, upper year students who have already been through the process, and where possible, professional career consultants. Résumés come in many different formats and sizes. There is no one way to write a résumé or cover letter. However, there are some guidelines to follow that will assist you in your drive for a summer job. Some of these are listed below:

> **Keep it Concise.** For those of you who have jumped from job to job, you may want to cut some of them out of your résumé, especially if they were short-lived or do not indicate your skills and abilities that will pertain to law. On the other hand, be sure to emphasize jobs where you have shown dedication and loyalty. These two items go a long way in making an impression.

Start Focussing on Law. Wherever possible and feasible, make connections to the field of law. Include any volunteering that you have done, or are doing, related to law. You will probably have opportunities to get involved in your first semester. Include these activities.

Set Yourself Apart. This probably seems obvious. However, candidates often overlook this idea. The truth of the matter is that recruitment is more about finding a good fit than in finding the perfect candidate. The résumé and cover letter process is the first step in getting yourself to the top of the pile. The pile is often large, so setting yourself apart early is very important. How can you set yourself apart? It is really a personal thing, but perhaps you could highlight your passionate reason for applying for law school, or highlight unique personal interests and hobbies such as involvement in sports or travel. What worked great for me was to create a professional personal website. I highlighted the URL address for this site in both my résumé and website. At the time, personal websites were rare, and many recruiters went to the website simply out of curiosity. When they arrived, they found all kinds of things about me that would never fit into a résumé, including photos, lists of awards and accomplishments, a more detailed résumé, etc. Often, I received positive feedback about my website at the time of the interview. Whatever your gimmick, make it unique, and if possible, fun. It is my opinion that if you can get yourself past the résumé cull, you are in fantastic shape, as you have already put yourself in the top 10 or 20 percent. I would suggest avoiding fancy paper, fonts, colours, etc. I am not convinced that any of that makes a difference. That opinion is based upon a tradition of stodginess. As I said, most recruiters are younger associates. You will have to use your instincts. If you feel that you are best represented on pink paper, then use pink paper. If you think that you want to incorporate modern, stylized design in your résumé, then do it. However, most people still use the old 20 lb white paper with Times New Roman or Arial font. If you want to get extreme, you may not want to work for a law firm that will reject you because of your personal style as represented on your résumé. Again, this is a grey area, and I do not feel qualified to tell you how to go about setting up your résumé. I am convinced, however, that unique = interview. "Unique" is different from "weird" and you need to be aware of the style of the firm. Show that *you* are unique, not just your résumé itself.

Do not Make Mistakes. Check everything over twice, then three times, then four. If possible, have others edit every copy of your résumé and cover letter that you send out. A misspelled firm or lawyer name can result in a toss into the garbage can for your résumé and/or cover letter. Also, be very sure that you have the address and postal code exactly right, and that the documents correspond with the envelope. Be sure that you have included sufficient postage, and make sure that your application will arrive in good time. If necessary, use an express service or courier. A late application is a missed opportunity.

I discuss suggestions for interviewing in greater detail in the section on the articling recruitment process.

For many of you, the opportunity to get far, far away from the law will be a welcome prospect upon completion of your first year final exams. You will likely feel a need to break free and try something different for four months. This is a very healthy thing. Contrary to many opinions, recruiters do not look down upon students who seek opportunities outside of the law, and will not, for the most part, punish them for doing so, at articling recruitment time. However, be sure that you can account for this time away from the law, and be able to explain why you did what you did. I had a classmate who went surfing all summer. I would be curious to hear the interview conversations that he had with recruiters. A non-law summer job can be a great opportunity to refresh your body and your mind. It can be a great opportunity to assess your first year, away from the crowd, competition and stress.

For others, you may want to explore areas or opportunities in law that are not a part of a law firm environment. There are many excellent opportunities in public law, legal research, and advocacy. As well, there are some awesome opportunities in the corporate realm. I will share my experience with you here, as this is what I chose to do with my first summer.

After failing to make the very competitive cut for summer positions at law firms, I decided to exploit any other legal contacts that I had. I applied for many positions posted with the career office at my law school. I also sent out emails to almost everybody that I knew indicating that I was looking for a summer job experience connected to the law. After many inquiries, one of my former friends put in a good word, along with my résumé, to the legal services department of the multinational oil company where he worked. This was a non-publicized position, and as a result, I was in a group of about ten applicants. This was pared down to three after the résumé sort, and I was able to successfully gain an offer for a summer position at this company.

The legal services department consisted of 16 well-seasoned lawyers with a large variety of expertise and interests. I worked at least once with each one of these lawyers on a large number of files. I wrote over 40 memorandums (many of them very concise) on at least 20 different areas of law, including employment law, labour law, Aboriginal law, contract law, oil and gas law, corporate governance, securities law, property law, municipal law, administrative law, privacy law, real estate law, international law, and more. I was able to attend some labour arbitrations, a hearing, and attended a number of legal consulting and client group meetings. I was the only summer student in the legal services department, and so was given a lot more attention than many of my classmates who were working at law firms. I was paid generously for a law summer student.

As well, there was little to no expectation to work overtime, so my summer was very manageable and enjoyable. Colleagues at law firms were often in the office long after the clock hit 5:00. I know some that even spent Saturdays at their firms. Not me. I was home every weekend, enjoying the summer rays.

You may think that if you do not get a summer job at a big or mid-sized law firm that you will be at a great disadvantage when it comes to articles. It is true, students who are hired for summer jobs make a good impression can avoid the articling process, thus enjoying less stress in their second year. However, these students are only filling a relatively small portion of the total article positions available to your particular class. As well, these students will not have the opportunity that you will have to explore the whole field. They will have only interviewed with those firms offering summer positions, which are usually few in number. For your article, you will have the opportunity to put out applications to many other firms and establishments, which ultimately might be to your advantage in gaining employment at a firm that is just right for you. Summer students often feel pressured into accepting an articling offer, as they do not want to gamble in the articling recruitment period. They would rather take a less-than-best article than no article at all.

By not summering at a big firm, you have a great opportunity to explore non-firm law related employment, such as research, advocacy, corporate or academic for example. Or, in turn, you can explore other interests, pursuits and opportunities.

Another great option for your summer is to study abroad. There are a number of fantastic chances to study an area of law of your choice in a destination of your choice, often with an excellent bursary attached. These programs are usually quite expensive, but you do usually get credit for your work there, which can take a big load off in your upper years of law school. Below are some examples of programs:

Montreal Summer Study Abroad
Villanova University School of Law - Study abroad without travelling too far from home.
http://www.law.villanova.edu/shared/montreal/montreal.asp

Queen's International Program
Britain (In a castle!) – (The Law of International Trade and Investment, International Commercial Arbitration, International Business Transactions) – http://www.queensu.ca /isc/academic/springsummer.html#ILP

The University of Pittsburgh School of Law and Semester at Sea
Offers you an incredible opportunity to travel to the Pacific Rim, studying the cultures and legal systems of seven countries. Departs from Vancouver. http://www.semesteratsea.com

Widener University School of Law - 2003 Summer International Law Institutes.
Four Summer International Law Institutes offered by Widener University School of Law – Nairobi, Kenya; Sydney, Australia; Geneva, Switzerland; and Venice, Italy – enable students to experience foreign cultures while learning from the different perspectives of students and faculty in foreign countries. These institutes offer a variety of courses and educational opportunities often unavailable in the United States. Students can earn up to six credits that may apply at their home law school. Both Widener Law and its summer programs are ABA-approved. Visit www.law.widener.edu, and click on International Program for more information.

As of the summer 2004, **Osgoode** hopes to provide special access to three summer programs:

(1) Mini-term of Monash University at its villa in Prato (just outside Florence)

(2) University of Montreal's China Law Summer Program in Beijing

(3) Trilater (Bologna, Osgoode, Monash) summer school in International Business Law in Bologna, Italy.

O. THE CANADIAN BAR ASSOCIATION (CBA)

As a law student, you have the opportunity to be a member of the Canadian Bar Association (CBA). For a nominal membership charge, you have the opportunity to attend numerous CBA events and lunch-hour seminars put on by CBA sections that focus on a large number of areas of law. Often the lunch is provided free, and the sessions prove to be very informative. These sessions can also be a great opportunity to network with practicing lawyers in a field of interest to you. As well, they are chances to explore different areas of law to see if they might interest you once you begin to practice. Another benefit of purchasing a student membership with the CBA is that you receive their publications, which are well written, and often informative about contemporary legal issues and issues facing Canadian lawyers. There are also opportunities to act as a student representative for the CBA. For more information go to http://www.cba.org.

P. EXECUTIVE POSITIONS IN LAW SCHOOL

Every law school will differ somewhat in their law student association or society. Our law school had a very robust and active Law Students' Association (LSA). There were many positions to fill for students in each year of law school. The LSA provided many useful and fun activities as well as information throughout the school year, including social events, commercial CANS, lockers, a student lounge, and a formal dinner and dance. Many students decide to get involved in this group to gain leadership experience, beef up their résumé, and to have fun during law school. Law school does not have to be all study and no fun, and our LSA made sure of this.

The process of elections for executive positions may intimidate you. It is not unlike elections in junior high or high school for the school executive. It can be a mad rush of getting nominated, putting up signs and photographs, preparing a speech, and doing any other type of self-promotion. This is not everyone's bag. This is especially true for first year students. You are facing many strangers in a strange and new environment.

As I was a bit shy, I looked for opportunities that did not involve speeches or elections per say. I ended up volunteering as a first-year representative for a couple of student groups and this led to being elected for executive positions for my second and third years. For me, this was a more safe and comfortable way to get involved. Recruiters looked very favourably on this type of activity, and I was able to be very involved with classmates and often with the community at large.

For many of us, law school will be the last formal post-secondary school that we go through. Why not have fun, get involved, and create some memories for yourself, all while polishing your résumé for those upcoming recruitment interviews?

Q. REGISTERING FOR 2L COURSES WHILE STILL IN 1L

Your first year of law school is pretty much laid out for you. But once you make it past that first year, you will be given a whole lot of freedom about the courses that you take. Some schools have certain required courses for upper years, and some even require certain courses in each of your second and third year. See the Course Requirement section of this book for details.

Even if you do have some required courses in upper years, for the most part you will have a lot of flexibility in your course choice. There are a number of considerations when choosing courses. The difficulty arises because you will have to register for second year courses in the waning months of your first year. You may still be unsure about what type of law you are interested in, what kind of firm or legal setting you want to end up in, or in a worst-case-scenario, what are of law you will do poorly in come exam time.

There are very different schools of thought regarding course choice in law school. One school suggests that you should stack your schedule with courses that will give you an edge for bar ad or CPLED courses. These often include the staples such as family, trusts, wills, real estate, etc. These areas of law will usually be covered on the bar exam or in your CPLED modules. However, you will cover these areas to such an extent that you should be well prepared for the exam or assignments, regardless of whether you took all of these types of classes. It would be unreasonable to expect every student to have taken all areas covered on the bar exam or in your CPLED courses, as this would negate the concept of a flexible course offering in your upper years. However, if you feel that there is an area of law that will intimidate you, and you want to get a jump-start on the subject area, perhaps consider registering for that class. Otherwise, I suggest that you do not sweat it too much.

Another school of thought, similar to that mentioned above, is that you should stack your schedule with courses that firms will find attractive. There is a belief by many that you should have all of the "staples" mentioned above, along with plenty of corporate classes if you are thinking of going into corporate law, criminal if you are thinking of going into criminal law, or torts if you are thinking of going into personal injury law, for example. Classmates will throw around the idea that you must absolutely take land titles, or judgment enforcement, or such types of classes. However, my experience during articling interviews was that it is not necessarily that important to have taken all of these "staple" courses. Recruiters realize that there simply is not enough time during your three years of law school to take every "ideal" course. They also realize that there are scheduling restrictions, and that you may not necessarily have a choice about taking certain classes. When I have asked about this problem, most recruiters have told me not to sweat it, and that the firm would ensure that I received instruction on any one particular area of law during my articling year, if required.

A third school suggests that you should simply take what you enjoy learning. Take a whole range of classes. You never know – you may discover an area of law that completely fascinates you. For example, I have a colleague who discovered international commercial arbitration. He had never even heard about the concept until he took a class on international business transactions, something that he had never intended to take but for a scheduling obstacle. Now he is fully pursuing the field. In any case, I believe that you should ensure that you do take at least some courses that are simply enjoyable, mind-expanding, or because you just love the style of the professor teaching the course. Law school should not be all about business. It is a wonderful opportunity to grow as an individual. Treat it as an extension of your liberal undergraduate education, and you will end up much more happy in the end.

Be sure that you will fulfill all credit requirements with your course choices. There have been nightmare stories of those who realized that they were one credit short come convocation registration time. Or more often, people can enter their last semester and end up having to take an extra class to meet credit requirements. This can be a real strain on what would have been otherwise a more relaxed or even pleasurable end to your law school career. Also, if you get educated in an area that interests you, you are more likely to practice the law that interests you.

Most schools offer a number of paper-based courses, or research projects. These can provide variety, and offer an opportunity to fine-tune legal research and writing skills, which will be valuable when you begin practicing. These can also ease exam-time strain, as you will already have completed your work before exam week comes. However, if you are a procrastinator, or if you have a hard time putting your thoughts down on paper, or if a 30 page or more project seems daunting to you, you may want to avoid these courses. Many people, ironically, prefer to get the course over in a two or three hour exam, even though there will be plenty of preparation time for that exam. I have always preferred paper courses because they often do not involve as much lecture time, they allow me to design a more flexible schedule, which can be very handy if you have a part-time job or other commitments. As well, a research project allows you to get a very firm grasp on a particular area of law, which can ultimately set you apart later down the road as someone who has expertise on a particular area of law. For example, I wrote a research paper on foreign corruption and bribery, and appropriate responses by Canadian multinational corporations. Who knows, this may be very valuable knowledge for a client some day down the road.

The timetable will indicate how each class section will be evaluated so you can choose a mix of courses based on more than the time of day. If you love to write, but 100% finals scare you, then look for options that have paper-based marks. Or, choose a mix so you don't have five papers or five finals.

You will also find a variety of pass/fail type courses, along with courses that involve presentations, role-play, or even internships. It is a good idea to take one or two of these types of courses to round out your experience, and to introduce you to a variety of skills, such as negotiation, client interviewing, court procedure and more.

R. ADVICE FROM 2LS AND 3LS

Many upper year students are willing to share their knowledge and experience with you. Take advantage of this opportunity when it arises. You will often gain exposure to upper year students through volunteer experiences. This is a great chance to get the goods on various things such as the moot, what professors are good, and what it is like to work at a firm or a non-profit organization. It is also a good chance to ask what courses they might recommend, to ask about study habits and legal research and writing techniques, and whatever else you can think of to give you an advantage in your law school experience.

I caution you to take advice or opinion from more experienced students with a filter in place. Remember that we are all individuals and react differently to various professors, classes, and situations. Try to canvass more than one person about any given topic, especially if you need to make a personal decision related to that topic. As well, avoid upper year students that show an obvious negative outlook on law school, particular professors, or areas of law. As I have said, surround yourself with positive people to have a positive experience at law school. You have enough challenge without someone painting a dismal picture for you of something that may prove to be a very positive experience for you. As a personal example, I can relate to you that even though an upper year student once told me that doing a moot competition would practically kill me and would leave me with a very bad taste for litigation, I persisted and participated in a moot. That moot ended up being one of the most positive experiences of my law school years. I never would have known how much I personally like the courtroom setting or preparing for litigation had I not experienced a competitive moot for myself. You really owe it to yourself to try as many different experiences as possible in your three years of law school. I was also told that there was no other good option beyond working at a national law firm for a summer job. I ended up working at a multinational corporation one year, and acting as Editor-in-Chief of the Alberta Law Review the next summer. I was not hurt in my own capacity to gain articling offers. In fact, the opposite was most likely true. On top of that, I gained incredibly valuable experience, enjoyed myself immensely, and got to do something that many other of my colleagues did not. Stretch your mind and embrace the opportunity to learn and grow. Do not limit yourself to what others say or do.

S. STUDENT LEGAL SERVICES

In my first year I signed up, along with a huge number of classmates, for a shift at Student Legal Services. This is a non-profit, student-run legal assistance program that provides legal services to low-income, underprivileged people on-campus or off-campus. There are a variety of similar organizations at various law schools in Canada (listed below). My experience was excellent, so I will take the opportunity make a plug for these organizations. I volunteered for both the criminal and civil sections. These were very different experiences. The criminal section required you to attend one shift per week at the SLS house, along with a small group of other students and two upper year student dayleaders. The office was open during this shift, and at any time, principals (clients) could come off the street to ask for legal advice. We were also responsible for answering the telephone and answering any questions that clients might have.

As a law student, you cannot provide legal advice. However, there is a monumental amount of *information* that you can provide, which can save the principal loads of time and, more importantly, money. Referrals can be made to Legal Aid, other low-income legal programs, legal information hotlines, etc. Where appropriate, we were also responsible for assisting the principal in preparing for court. As a law student (or actually anyone), you can represent the principal in a summary proceeding, such as traffic violations, bylaw tickets, etc. as their agent. You cannot represent principals for indictments, or other higher-level charges, such as assault, robbery, etc.

I was able to assist principals in preparing their files for their upcoming court dates. This involved interviewing the principal and getting full information into their file, obtaining any evidence that would be in the principal's favour, filing and submitting any necessary legal documentation to the court, and meeting with a lawyer to discuss the matter. Lawyers volunteered their time to discuss matters with students on a weekly basis.

When it came time for court, I was able to assist the principal in walking through the procedure (i.e. where to sit, what to say, how to address the court, how to bow when entering and exiting, etc.). I spoke to the court on the principal's behalf, indicating that I was a law student with Student Legal Services. For the most part, the judge and the lawyers representing the prosecution were very kind and gentle with me, and walked me through anything that I was unfamiliar with. It can be very intimidating as a first year law student to stand up in court and try to advocate something or represent information in such a formal setting. However, it was one of the most rewarding and learning-rich experiences of my law school career, and I would recommend it to anyone, whether you are interested in litigation or not. For me, the experience confirmed my desire to be involved in litigation in some way.

Those who really like their Student Legal Services experience may have the opportunity to apply for a full-time summer position. If you have an interest in criminal law or civil litigation in general, this is an excellent opportunity to learn, gain experience, and make good contacts. It can also lead towards becoming a dayleader for Student Legal Services, which is also an excellent opportunity to gain further practical experience.

The civil law section differed somewhat in that I spent most of my time on the telephone. Like with the criminal section, I was responsible for providing information. However, with this section, a seasoned dayleader who was either a law professor or a practitioner was available each shift. If an answer was too difficult to answer myself, I could put the client on hold and ask the dayleader for the answer. Most of the time, we were able to point the principal in the right direction. Every once in a while, a principal would come into the office and we would help them to prepare documentation. Examples of principal matters were small claims court applications, landlord/tenant issues, and separation and divorce matters. We were able to write and send demand letters on behalf of the principal, which in many cases was very effective in getting the desired result. SLS also conducted do-your-own-divorce clinics, which we would refer telephone callers to attend.

It amazed me how much more easily I was able to address questions by the end of the school year, compared with the first time that I answered a phone call. Down times also provided an opportunity to talk about the ins and outs of law school with 2L and 3L students, opportunities that 1L's rarely have. Again, I learned a ton and had a lot of fun. I cannot recommend this experience enough!

Alberta – Student Legal Services (Criminal and Civil sections) (http://www.lslap.bc.ca/)

UBC – Law Students' Legal Advice Program (LSLAP) (http://www.lslap.bc.ca/)

Calgary – Student Legal Assistance (http://www.fp.ucalgary.ca:8030/SLA/)

Dalhousie – Dalhousie Legal Aid Services (http://www.dal.ca/~wwwlaw/clinic/gi.html)

Toronto – Downtown Legal Services
(http://www.dls.utoronto.ca/default.html)

Osgoode – C.L.A.S.P – Community and Legal Aid Services
Programme
(http://www.yorku.ca/osgoode/clasp/claspgen.htm)

Ottawa – Legal Clinic
(http://www.uottawa.ca/associations/clinic/)

Queen's – Queen's Legal Aid
(http://law.queensu.ca/students/Legal_Aid/index.php)

Western Ontario – Community Legal Services

T. DO I NEED A LAPTOP?

More and more students are using laptops in law school. In my last semester, I took a random count near the end of the term, and counted 54% of the class with laptops during a lecture. In comparison, the count was about 25% at the beginning of the semester. UVic did a survey in 2003, and about 72% of their incoming students had laptops and just over 50% of those laptops were wireless. Many of my classmates came to realize the advantages of having a laptop in law school, and decided to bite the bullet and get one.

I had a laptop throughout law school. The reasons for me were plentiful. I type far faster than I can take notes by hand. It also allowed me to keep my head up, looking at the professor during the lecture. This in turn allowed me to keep tabs on him or her, which can be very important in a Socratic style lecture. I could read the professor and better anticipate when I might be called upon to provide an answer.

All students should prepare notes for their upcoming lectures. Those with laptops can have some advantage over their laptop-less counterparts during the lecture. With a laptop, you can quickly scroll to information that the professor is referring to. You can use the search function to seek out in your personal notes the facts of a particular case by typing in a keyword. Further advantages come after the lecture is over. I also kept numerous CANS that I found on the Internet, that I collected from classmates, or that were sold commercially by our Law Students' Association. With my laptop in front of me, I was able, if necessary, to do quick searches for a particular case being covered in class, while in class, and many times incorporated what I found in that search into my class notes. Or when I was totally stumped, I could refer to this myriad of information with a very quick search function query. It saved me more than once. On one occasion, I even did a quick search on the Internet during a lecture, as I had been less prepared than I would have liked.

In my law school, we had high-speed Internet access at most seats in the lecture halls. There is now wireless Internet access throughout the law faculty, so if you have a wireless card for your laptop, you can have access to the Internet anywhere. This is great for lectures, but is also invaluable when you are studying or writing papers.

There is further advantage to having a laptop post-lecture. I was able to swap notes with classmates many times immediately after the lecture. I have also spent many hours right after a lecture going over the notes that I just completed, and filling in the gaps using my collection of CANS, the Internet, and textbooks or class materials if necessary.

Having a laptop while doing research or writing papers is invaluable. This allows you to do your work in the law library at your school, providing great convenience and time-savings. You will spend a good amount of time searching through the stacks of books, and it is great to avoid having to sign books out to take home, or to have to write your research notes by hand.

I purchased a used laptop during my first year, and it was more than sufficient. As long as you have a word processor, and access to the Internet (high speed is preferable), you are off to the races. Later on, I purchased a very good new laptop for $999, and it is what I used to write this book. I would not be without a laptop in law school if I were you.

I balance this advice with some words of caution. Not everyone can afford a laptop. As well, some people cannot type very fast. If this describes you, please ignore the above. Many of my classmates made it through law school just fine without a laptop. As well, I have heard many times that exam writing can be compromised if you only write things using a keyboard. Law exams are brutal endurance writing experiences, and if your hand and wrist are not accustomed to writing at lightning speed for up to three hours at a time, you may want to come up with a plan to wean yourself from your laptop for a while prior to exam time. I utilized this technique in my third semester as my wrists killed for a week after my first year finals. I have also chosen to take notes by hand for one class each semester just to keep my wrist in shape. This was not on purpose. There were no plug-in outlets in that particular classroom, and my laptop would always run out of power before the lecture ended. But I have found this to be a valuable exercise for exam time.

Another caveat – if you think you will be prone to play solitaire or surf the web during class, avoid a laptop. Unfortunately, this includes many people. I always marvelled at how many people spent their classes playing solitaire, with the knowledge of how much those people had paid in tuition to attend that particular class. If you think you might have a problem with this, delete solitaire or any other distracting material from your computer. Likewise, you may want to keep your wireless card or Ethernet cable at home or in your bag.

I also purchased voice recognition software for my computers. This has saved valuable time, as I can "type" the equivalent of about 140 words per minute with this software. I do have to go back and edit for errors, but the errors decrease the more one uses the software. I have used this technique for writing papers, and for preparing my final CANS. It is great to be able to have your hands free to flip through textbooks, class materials and other sets of notes, and to simply speak into the microphone headset. This may be the ticket for you if you are a seek-and-peck typist.

A Word from the Wise – Practical Experience

Did I use a laptop? Yes, and no. I brought a laptop to school to make my own notes and work on papers, but I didn't use one in class. I would only recommend using one in class if you type fast.
— Mike Kariya, University of Calgary

I purchased a laptop about 3 months into law school and feel it was a great purchase. I can type much clearer and faster than I can write and therefore it has improved my notes considerably. Before purchasing a laptop I would take my notes home after classes and type them into the computer so I would be able to read them easier in the future. I would recommend to anyone to purchase a laptop for school.
— Jaime Johnson, University of Alberta

I did not use a laptop in law school. If you are a strong typist, then a laptop may be helpful in taking notes. I, however, found writing my notes and then coming home and typing them was a great review of the lecture and what I had just learned. If I had a laptop, I don't think I would have had such a regular review of the materials.
— Lorne Randa, University of Alberta

U. Textbooks – Used? New?

Why would you pay retail price for something that you could purchase for 50% off or less? Until third year, when I received a sponsorship for textbooks and materials, I bought as many textbooks as possible in lightly used condition. I had no difficulty in obtaining textbooks with relatively little mark-up in them. When there was highlighting or underlining, I usually found it useful to my studies, as it helped me to locate important information quickly upon first reading. I tried to avoid textbooks that were heavily marked-up, and I flipped through each book to get a sense of what type of student owned the book before I bought the book.

You may argue that you like the feel of a nice, crisp textbook, and that you like to make all of your own mark-ups to the textbook. If that is your bag, go for it. However, for most of us, saving a few bucks (or a few hundred in this case) is very desirable. Most law schools provide some method of obtaining used textbooks. Some have used textbook sales each fall. Some sell used textbooks through the regular university book store. If these methods do not work for you, do not worry – there will be plenty of signs on bulletin boards around the law school.

If you can, try to find someone who took a lot of the same classes as you and see if you can buy a "set" of textbooks from them for a "package" price. They will probably be glad to get rid of them all at one time, and will be likely to give you a discounted price.

V. Pro Bono Work

Pro bono work is something that a lawyer, or in your case a law student, offers free of charge. Many practicing lawyers have a pro bono component to their practice, as a good faith service to the community, and pro bono work can be requisite of being a professional. A lawyer may take on a particular client, or will do pro bono consulting work for a non-profit organization.

Many Canadian law schools have some sort of pro bono law student organization. Some of these organizations are very well organized and provide a prolific amount of volunteer service to a large number of non-profit establishments and individuals. According to the Pro Bono Students Canada Website, work can range from "research[ing] legal issues relevant to the organisation or their clients, contribut[ing] to advocacy work on behalf of the organisation, produc[ing] reports and policy papers, re-draft[ing] board policy and manuals, review[ing] new materials (Internet, recent case law, periodicals etc), update[ing] resources, perform[ing] legal education, such as writing brochures or presenting workshops, provid[ing] legal support and information to clients or an organisation, [and] assist[ing] in intakes and assessments."[4]

Doing pro bono work is a fantastic opportunity to get involved in the community, practice legal research, writing and education in a practical situation, and is a great way to build up your personal résumé with practical legal experiences. For more information, see http://www.law.utoronto.ca/probono /main_e.htm.

W. STUDY HABITS

The only reason some people get lost in thought is because it's unfamiliar territory.
— Paul Fix

---

[4] http://www.slsedmonton.com/pbsc/org.html.

a. Reading Textbooks

In an ideal world, all law students would complete all of their assigned readings. Preferably, law students should keep up to date on all cases that are being discussed in a subsequent class, as this would allow one to follow the instructor more easily and feel confident when called upon. I have to admit up front that I am a poor spokesman for completing all law school readings. I would like to tell you that I diligently read the 40-70 pages assigned each day in law school. I would like to tell you that I then diligently briefed all of the cases that I read, went to class the next day, then summarized and revisited my notes after class, and then began the cycle again. I have read some books that have advised this practice. I am sure that there are some students who are able to achieve this monumental feat. However, I believe that they are very rare indeed. A colleague of mine who attended a relatively small law school once did an informal survey of classmates in his third year of law school and found only one individual who could claim to have achieved the above description. Suffice it to say, this individual received exemplary marks.

I also must tell you that those who achieve something resembling the above description often are at the higher end of grades. I warn you that most students in law school do not regularly succeed in completing all readings assigned. Nor do they successfully brief all of their cases in time for the next class. Nor do they regularly go back to modify their previously prepared notes based on their classroom experience. The truth is that many law students scramble all semester long, cramming in their efforts at the end of the semester, collecting as many CANS or outlines as they can, and meeting with classmates in a last-ditch effort to comprehend the information that will help them to write the final exam.

I can relate to you in a retrospective manner about the experiences that I had in my three years of law school, and share with you what worked for me and what did not work for me. Beyond that, there are some other good sources out there that may be able to help you to increase your ability to organize yourself during the semester, and to increase your chances for success on law exams. I have the benefit of being able to reflect upon three years of law school, and its corresponding examination schedule. Hindsight is 20/20, theoretically, and I should be able to share with you some wisdom that may help you, especially through the tough times.

If there is one thing that I can relay to you as a law graduate, it is this: BE CONSISTENT! I All-Caps those two words, because I cannot emphasize the importance of those two words enough. In your undergraduate studies, you probably had one or two midterms, some assignments, some labwork, a presentation or two, all depending on your faculty, and upon your semester. You probably had a mixture of multiple choice, short answer, and occasionally an essay question on your exams. Well, in law school these things, for the most part, do not exist anymore. You now face, in your first year especially, 100% written, long-form exams. Often, they are closed-book exams. Those that are open-book tend to be more challenging; so do not think that you are off the hook when you read in your syllabus that your exam is open book.

This new regime of 100%, fact pattern-based examination can be a complete shock to the uninitiated. It can also be extremely intimidating. It was for me. But I survived, and I learned a lot along the way. The first thing that I learned is that this method of testing requires absolute, resolute self-discipline. There is just no way that you can cram an entire semester worth of information into one session, or even a week. You will not feel very confident going into the exam room if you choose to take this route. There is a reason why I found a direct correlation between those individuals listed on the Dean's List and those individuals who I routinely found studying long hours in the law library. They were consistent. They had self-discipline. They had a plan, they stuck to it, and as a result, they were prepared when it came to exam time.

So, how long should you be studying? How long should you be reading? There is no formula out there that lends itself towards success. From my experience, the more important consideration is the quality of your study sessions, and the consistency of those quality study sessions. To achieve your best results, you need to begin your plan of attack on the first day of each semester, and lay out what needs to be done to fully comprehend the vast amount of information before you.

So, in relation to doing all of your readings, even if you are unable to complete all of your readings (likely), you should aim to have an adequate number of regular and consistent study sessions each week. Do not deviate from this plan. Even if you don't get everything read, at the very least you will, be working throughout the semester on building concept upon concept into your arsenal, and you will find that come cram-time, you will be largely prepared. Don't get bogged down and frustrated that you cannot ever complete your reading assignments. Do your best to meet this goal, but be more concerned that you at least spend a consistent amount of time EVERY DAY of EVERY WEEK. Give yourself rewards if you like. Here is the bottom line: you cannot make up lost time in law school. There just is not enough time to spare in any given week. Stay consistent, and improve your chances for success in a very big way.

The above advice assumes that you will not be able to get all of your reading done. So, what reading should you be sure to get done, and what should you do with that information once you have read it? I found that in almost all cases that I learned a great deal, or the information stuck much better in my brain, if I prepared for class. That means that I at least skimmed the headnote (i.e. summary) of each case or chapter that I was supposed to read BEFORE I attended class. It also meant that I, at the very least, recorded the basics of each case or concept beforehand as well. Now, I did not always achieve this. I am just saying that when I did, the benefits of attending class were much enhanced. Equally, if I spent even a marginal amount of time each day going over the pre-class notes that I prepared and the notes that I took during class, and filled in any gaps in either of these, the information stayed with me much better, I was able to make important connections between legal concepts as we went along, and I was a lot less stressed as the end of the semester approached.

Reading cases will take up the majority of your reading time. Cases can tend to be very long, sometimes very poorly written, and most often do not come to the point quickly. They are advanced legal analysis, often written after much study, research and deliberation. You will find that it takes a lot of practice to be able to read between the lines, to find the important stuff quickly. The more you do practice, the easier it gets.

Fortunately, many tools out there can help you cut through the loads of information. Get a hold of the best quality CANS or outlines that you can. As well, use online services such as Quicklaw™ or Westlaw™ to find case summaries. These are especially useful if you find that you have run out of time. However, I encourage you to prepare to the best of your ability and time constraints for each class. Again, BE CONSISTENT. Your brain works best if it has time to digest information and to make as many connections as possible. Don't fall into a trap of just reading other people's CANS or outlines and never reading cases because you need to practice transferring what you read in fact patterns and legal analysis to the practical application of the law.

My second piece of advice for readings is regularly annotate the information that you have learned into your own CAN or outline. Readings, or for that matter, summaries or case briefs, are worth nothing if you cannot integrate the information, summarize it in a manner that is understandable and meaningful to you in the most concise manner possible. This will also take a huge load off you when it comes time to really hit the books in preparation for those exams.

A Word from the Wise – Practical Experience

I did not do all my readings. I skipped the really long cases and read summaries instead.
— Rob Nelson, Queen's University, University of Calgary transfer student

In first year, I did most of my readings. Since then the extent of my reading has declined. I think that when you are reading a case one must remember that they are chosen by the professor to illustrate a specific principle, so try not to let yourself get bogged down in extraneous aspects of the case. Remember the principle of the case and the basic facts but don't stuff your mind with all the twists and turns of the case because you will not have the time to explain them on the exam anyway, unless of course the professor says that you may have to write a case comment. Also it is worth pointing out that over time some cases have come to stand for certain principles, which on closer reading are not exactly what the case says. If you come across this, don't twist your mind into knots trying to logically reconcile two irreconcilable interpretations; just remember the principle that the case is supposed to stand for.
— Robin Penker, University of Alberta

I only know one person who completed all readings. I usually did the readings in smaller classes where there was a strong likelihood of being called upon.
— Shawn Davis, University of Calgary LLB/MBA
In most of my classes, I kept up with all the readings. If I was unable to complete the readings, I would at least try to read a case summary or head note in order to get a basic understanding of the case and its relevance.

In terms of selecting readings, if a professor recommends a case as being important, I would at least read that case in its entirety. If the course was a paper-based course, I tended not to read anything unless it related to an assignment that I had. As well, I would skip reading a case if I had already read it in a prior class.

— Lorne Randa, University of Alberta

When it came to crunch time, I skipped all course readings related to "historical" or "US approach" or "UK approach" etc. and just focused on what would be directly relevant for exams.

— Mike Kariya, University of Calgary

I didn't do all my readings for class. I generally decided by starting a course doing as much of the readings as was possible. As a course went on I generally continued the readings that were more beneficial when accompanied with lectures and less reading on concepts that were being explained fully without as much need for the readings. Alternatively, I read most of the material that was required for classes where professors would ask specific students questions during lectures.

— Jaime Johnson, University of Alberta

I didn't read absolutely everything but I liked to read as much as possible. If I didn't have time to read everything, I used the professor's lectures as a guide as to what the important cases were and then I read those.

— Kim Yee, University of Alberta

X. APPLY FOR 1L SUMMER JOB

Please see Chapter 6 for a full outline on what to consider for your 1L summer job. What I want to say here is that you need to be prepared in advance. Get your résumé and cover letter prepared very early in the school year. As well, do your research on firms as early as possible. Lastly, get help with interviewing skills. Interviews with law firms are somewhat different than interviews elsewhere. Get help from your career officer and from colleagues (especially in upper years) through mock interviews. Lastly, take every opportunity to make contacts in the legal community. These can be made through organized events, conferences, etc. You may also consider asking firms that you are interested in for the opportunity to have a tour of the firm, and to conduct a survey interview. You may also find an opportunity to shadow a lawyer from that firm.

Y. CANNING!

No doubt, you will hear all about CANS during your first weeks of law school. Professors will ward you off them. upper year students will tell you to get a good one. You will scramble to find them. What is a CAN you ask? CANS are Condensed Annotated Notes. Some people call them outlines. Basically, they are the particular law class in a nutshell.

Most CANS or outlines follow a set skeleton or standard: Facts, Ratio, Analysis (or Reasoning), and Conclusion (or Held). The facts provide a brief description of what transpired in the case at hand, for both the plaintiff and the defendant. They describe the most important facts related to the problem at hand. They do not usually include extraneous facts that do not lend themselves to the decision to be made by the trier of fact (judge or jury). The *ratio* is a Latin concept that means "The principle or rule of law on which a court's decision is founded, or The rule of law on which a later court thinks that a previous court founded its decision; a general rule without which a case must have been decided otherwise" (Black's Law Dictionary). The Analysis is a quick summary of the reasoning of the court. In some cases, it may be more detailed, depending on the complexity of the facts. The Conclusion is the outcome of the case.

a. Do Your Own CAN!

As I said above, if you find the very best CAN in the world for a particular course, you will want to create your very own, from scratch; CAN before you hit the exam room. You may think that you can get away without this step (and there may be a few of you out there who can do this), but for most of us, this is a necessary step in the learning, synthesizing and memorizing process. By physically writing your own review notes, you will most likely be able to recall information more quickly and efficiently. This is especially true for closed-book exams. For open-book exams, writing your own CAN will allow you to be more familiar with the information, and you will be able to flip more quickly through your notes during the exam.

I have always found writing a CAN from scratch after studying my class notes and other materials to be an invaluable exercise to help me see where I am. I start with a fresh piece of paper or computer screen, and simply write out as much of the course as I am able to in as little space as possible. I include all relevant cases, statutes, and supplementary information as possible, all the while trying to make as many links in the information as possible. I try to remember why a particular case or statute is important in the big picture, whether it has altered or developed the law, and what the potential problems or solutions might be as a result of the reasoning of the case or statute. I may include some personal comments about where I think this case or statute may come up in an exam question, or write myself little notes that will help me to readily recall a piece of information come exam time. Whatever helps, I include it. I try to keep it as concise as possible, while trying not to omit potentially important information. This is a tough balance to strike, and it may take you a few times to get it figured out. The important thing is to avoid relying upon other people's work in hopes that it will get you by. The truth of the matter is that it usually will only just get you by, or slightly less. To succeed, there is no better alternative than putting in that effort and making it happen for yourself.

A Word from the Wise – Practical Experience

Unless you have a very bad and disorganized professor and you have to teach yourself the course, other people's CANs are not the best or most efficient way to learn a course because it is actually the creation of the CAN that helps you learn the material much more than simply studying someone else's. That said, it is better to read a commercial CAN or someone else's CAN than nothing at all.
— Robin Penker, University of Alberta

To prepare for law school exams I would go through my notes and create my own "CAN". Once that was finished, I would compare that to the commercial CAN and look for discrepancies. The next step was to create a list of cases from the course with a one-line explanation of the ratio. When I started, I would spend less time organizing and more time trying to study by reading the notes repeatedly. As school progressed, I found it more effective to spend much more time organizing notes and continuously revising them as I studied.
— Jaime Johnson, University of Alberta

b. Three Kinds of CANS

Every law student will develop their own way of compiling information for exam purposes. Because most law courses will have a 100% final exam, or something almost as substantial, it is a very important skill to be able to compile a lot of information very efficiently. This can be a difficult chore, as you will read loads and loads of very dense cases and statutes, and will be thrown tons of information during lectures. You will work hard to have enough information at hand to be prepared for class, but will then want to pare that information to the bare bones concepts so that it is easy to recall and apply to the problems in your exams. There are many ways to compile a good CAN. I have come up with my own strategy that has worked for me, so I share it with you here as an example.

I often created three sets of CANS for each class. The first, which I call Daddy Bear (I have kids, obviously), is a complete set of notes that includes information that I gathered from other CANS, notes that I made while reading cases in preparation for class, information that I gathered at the lecture, and lastly any subsequent thoughts or information that I added after each class. This ended up being a very dense, very thick document. It is not an appropriate study tool, unto itself, and is not an appropriate document to bring into an exam, if it is an open-book exam. However, it is a great tool for weekly review sessions, and it is the first thing that I read at the beginning of exam preparation time. It provided a lot of detail, and usually did not have many gaps, if I had done all of my preparation and post-class work. It was also a useful document for sharing with classmates who had missed a class or two, or who did not understand a particular concept. They could then sift through and make heads or tails of the information themselves.

The second CAN that I prepared, which I called Mama Bear, is a pared down version of Papa Bear. It included only the very relevant facts, reasoning, *ratio*, analysis and conclusion for all case law studied. It also included the most important statute law, any important definitions, and any key thoughts from the professor. It included enough detail to jog my memory while I was studying. I brought this CAN to open-book exams, not as a primary tool, but as a back-up tool.

The CAN that I relied upon for open-book exams, and which I used for study in the last days before a closed-book exam, was the Baby Bear. This was basically a fact sheet that provided the bare bone information, key links between cases, key definitions in short form, and key statutes. I usually did not include more than 2-3 lines of information for each case; less if possible. I often only included key words that would jog my memory. If I was struggling to remember something, I could always pull out Mama Bear.

So, why all the work? Actually, it ends up being a lot less work than it would seem. The Papa Bear is like the encyclopaedia for the course. It has everything. Creating Mama Bear is simply a matter of culling the information in Papa Bear. This process is great because it really forces you to decide what is most important, and to make key links in the information. By the time you get to Baby Bear, you should already be so familiar with the information and concepts that you are really just creating a sort of "cheat sheet" for yourself.

Everyone has their own way of dealing with the vast amount of information presented to them. This way helped me to deal with it.

Another technique that I have used is to design a flowchart that includes every important concept or rule that we have learned in a course. I try to fit this onto two or three written sheets of paper. I then have written that information more than once and as with the three bears, forced myself to write as much as possible by memory before copying out the rest. I did not stop this rewriting and memorizing process until I had fully learned by heart all of the information contained in those sheets. I then, on some closed-book exams, wrote out the entire two or three sheets during the exam as a tool for myself. I have even handed that information in along with my exam (in the exam booklet), not necessarily because it answered the exam problem, but because it demonstrated my mastery of the information. This may not be advantageous to you, and not all professors will appreciate this technique. But for me, as I have a relatively poor memory, it helped me to get my bearings during an exam, and to feel more confident about being able to tackle the legal problems on exams.

Other people create case flow charts, where they will chart out the entire course on a large single piece of paper. This can be very useful for seeing the development of the law in that area of law.

c. Commercial Cans

If your Law Students' Association or Society is a good one, they will produce and sell commercial CANS at your law school. These CANS are usually solicited from upper year students or graduates. Usually a modest amount of money is offered by the LSA for the best CAN submitted. These in turn are edited and formatted for consistency and then sold to students for a nominal charge that includes the printing cost and a little bit more. The sale of CANS is often used as a fundraiser for student activities later in the year.

The quality of these CANS can differ greatly from class to class and author to author. My advice is that it cannot hurt for you to purchase a set of commercial CANS like those described above. I have had ones that mimicked the lecturer almost word for word. Others have included far too much information, others not enough.

You will receive fair warning from most professors that you should not rely upon commercial CANS, and that they can be a real detriment to you. If there is one thing that all professors DO NOT like, it is regurgitated CANS information on exams. Do not rely solely upon commercial CANS. I have heard some urban myths about students who did not study for an exam, other than reading the commercial CAN the night before, and who met with success. But, this is a rare story, and one that is hard for me to believe.

A commercial CAN, for the most part, can give you a good overall perspective on the course material, especially case law. They can also help greatly in preparation for those Socratic method lecturers who will drill you on facts, conclusions, and everything in between. The best thing to do is to use the commercial CAN as a beginning place, and use it to augment your own prepared CAN, and your class preparation.

A Word from the Wise – Practical Experience

I did find the commercial CANS generally useful for two purposes. I would use them to find what material was missed when I was absent from a lecture, and to compare to my own notes for accuracy before an exam.
— Jaime Johnson, University of Alberta

d. Online Resources

I include these resources with caution. I have found many outlines from schools other than my own extremely useful in my studies, but it can be easy to get bogged down by the vast number available, and can be time consuming to go through each looking for useful information. However, I found it useful to download as many as I could for each subject I was currently studying and using my search function on my laptop to look for particular cases. This would bring up each CAN that was relevant in a window; I could quickly open each of them up and scan for the best outline of the case at hand. I do not recommend doing this process in class. You may find yourself overwhelmed, confused, or not paying attention. It is best to do this preparation before class.

These outlines can also be useful in gauging your own CAN that you SHOULD be building yourself, and will give you a good idea of what works for you and what does not. Some people like a lot of detail; others only want the fundamentals when it comes to exam preparation.

Below are some good sources for obtaining CANS from various schools. You can also access all of my CANS, along with others that I have collected along the way, at my website www.canadalawstudent.ca/cans.html.

UVic Law Student Resources – Student Outlines
http://outlines.law.uvic.ca/
Lots of first year and upper year CANS, updated yearly.

Queen's Law Students Outlines Site
http://qsilver.queensu.ca/~lss/outlines/
By far the most comprehensive site, with the best quality CANS, in my opinion.

University of Calgary – Women in Law
CANS – http://www.fp.ucalgary.ca/womeninlaw/
A large selection of first, second and third year CANS

UBC Law Students' Association CANS
http://faculty.law.ubc.ca/cans/
CANS provided on an as-is basis. Very good site.

Ed Chan – Outlines
http://www.edchan.ca/outlines.htm
Intended for University of Manitoba Students, but some very useful CANS for every law student.
Melanie's Law Notes
http://www.geocities.com/melanie_lawnotes/
A few good sets of notes here.

Duhaime Law
http://www.duhaime.org/

This is not an outline site per se, but is a great resource for various courses. I used it extensively for contract law. It also has a great legal dictionary.

Peter Carver – Constitutional Law
http://www.law.ualberta.ca/courses/carver/constitution/
A good resource for constitutional law.

Z. PRACTICE EXAMS

> *It wasn't raining when Noah built the ark.*
> — Howard Ruff

There has been no other single thing more valuable to my success in law school than doing practice exams. Get a hold of as many as you can. Try to get past exams given by the professor that you have, along with exams from other professors or instructors. Exams from other schools can be useful as well. Often, you will be able to access these exams online at your school, or from your law library, where they are kept in bound editions. Find out where you can access these exams as soon as possible, and start collecting them. You may like to try taking an exam midway through the course just to get a feel for how the professor will try to test you. It will also provide an opportunity to see your weaknesses in content and analysis. Doing a practice exam early on will open your mind to particular questions or problems, and can cause you to ask better questions of your professor in class or out of class, and to notice more subtle aspects of the cases that you read.

In preparation for exams, complete as many practice exams as possible. For open-book exams, write using your personally prepared CAN. This will show you where you have gaps in your CAN, and where you need to augment information or analysis skills. At least once or twice (especially before first year exams), simulate the exam-writing environment. Keep strict track of the time, and, if possible, write it at the same time of the day as you will be writing the actual exam. Bring the same snacks or drinks that you plan to bring to the exam. This will help you to better prepare for your physical needs, and will help you to relax when you enter the examination room on exam day. You will already be familiar with the process and the demands that will be placed on you.

Many professors are willing to review your answers to past exams. They may help you to identify where you have gone wrong, will provide exam writing suggestions and strategies, and will usually illuminate a particular fact, reasoning or analysis from a case that you have studied. Remember, it is their job to teach you the law, not only to test you on the law. You are not just paying tuition to enjoy the luxury of listening to a lecture and to be examined. You are in law school to learn the law, contrary to the belief of many rather egotistical legal academics. Since you are the future of the law system, the responsibility falls upon the law professors and instructors to develop the best lawyers possible. Be sure to schedule times to meet with professors or instructors well in advance of the exam. Provide yourself enough time to tackle the problems you are facing, and to go back to the exams you have written to see where you have gone wrong. If possible, try writing another practice exam after you have met with the professor or instructor.

You may be intimidated by the prospect of writing a bunch of practice exams. However, in my experience, this step of the learning process is crucial to your success. It took me two years to learn this lesson. My results in 2L were far superior, and the one thing that contributed most was writing numerous practice exams. By the time that I wrote the actual exam, I was already a pro at identifying issues in a problem and in analyzing and coming up with an intelligent conclusion.

AA. STUDY GROUPS

Study groups can be very helpful or they may be a large time sucker.

I personally did not find study groups to be useful, with some exceptions. For the most part, I found that study groups were disorganized and difficult to schedule. Many times, members of study groups would show up unprepared, bogged down by other pressures. Conversation tended to veer from exam content to professors, job stuff, other students, what was on TV the night before, and so on. This was the last thing that I wanted to subject myself to during a very stressful approach towards exam time.

That said, I did find a few students who were very focused on exam preparation, and who were very accountable in their preparation for study group meetings. I tried to meet at least once before exams each semester. In some cases, I met two or three times. Once a week for 2-3 weeks before exam time seemed to be appropriate and manageable.

During study group meetings, write a practice exam question for the other person, and then both answer it right there during the meeting. Then compare your answers and fill any gaps that you can identify in the other person's answer. Also do this exercise with existing past exam questions.

Another technique is to describe to the other person the entire course in about 10 minutes, linking one concept to the next, mentioning key cases along the way. This is a great technique for synthesizing the information from the course, locking in key concepts and case names and facts into your mind. It has also been proven that teaching someone else results in far superior personal retention of information.

The key thing during study group meetings is to prepare, to focus, and to have purpose. If what you are doing will not help you to increase your score on the final exam, you should be doing something else. Your time is far too valuable to waste on idle chitchat or gossip.

That said, you should definitely make some time for socializing during your exam preparation period. By doing so, you will provide yourself a potential reward for diligently studying the rest of the time. It will act as a great outlet for stress. Try to keep conversation light. Do not get bogged down in details, and stay away from negative talk. Conversation should be full of encouragement for each other. Keep these appointments brief, and during a time when you find that your attention often dwindles, such as 3:00 – 4:00 pm. Another option is to hit the gym, go for a run, or do some other entertaining activity with a friend to let off some steam.

A Word from the Wise – Practical Experience

I used study groups in my first and second year, but not so much in my third year. I used them mostly around exam period and found them usually quite useful. I would definitely recommend them because they usually help to clarify things and help in getting a full analysis of hypothetical exam question (everyone sees things differently, and hopefully that brings out all the issues in a question). I would assume that a study group throughout a term would also be beneficial and time-efficient in reviewing course material.
— Lorne Randa, University of Alberta

Small study groups are very effective. If you get two or three friends and go through the course, after everyone has prepared, you will discover those areas that you missed or those areas that you are weak in. The one danger of study groups is that if they get too big, everyone wants to have his or her say and it

takes forever to get through the material. The period before exam time is precious so don't waste it!
— Robin Penker, University of Alberta

BB. EXERCISE – SO IMPORTANT!

You may think that this section does not apply to you. You may think that you do not have time or energy now to exercise, so why would you have time during law school, when you will already be so busy. If you really, truly believe this, then skip this section and read on.

Making time for exercise, even if it is very moderate exercise will do wonders for you during law school. I am a huge advocate of making exercise a priority. I cannot speak for all of my classmates, but I know that for myself, my productivity with schoolwork went down dramatically when I did not make time for a workout on a regular basis. Exercise can help you in a number of ways. First, it allows you to take some time for yourself, to feed your body something that is good for it. It allows you to get away from the stress of case briefing, study groups, and the general mêlée of law school. It allows you to see another part of the campus, which is rare because you will be taking your classes all in the same building during law school. Exercise also gives you stamina and energy later on, especially during exam preparation time and during exams. As well, because you will be forced to sit in a desk chair for so many hours every day, establishing some muscle base will allow you to continue to burn calories, even while you are stationary.

I chose to workout three to four times per week for 1 hour per day during my first two years of law school. I tried to go with a friend as often as possible. This kept me accountable, and provided some much needed social interaction, which I felt deeply deprived of. During my last year, I chose to train for a triathlon, something I had been wanting to do for years, and for which I felt I had more time to concentrate on with a lighter course load and less anxiety about finding a job.

There are many other opportunities to be active. Our law school had a running club. They also had a rugby club, and quite a few intramural teams. We also had a yoga club. Many of my classmates worked out at the gym, got involved in intramurals on their own, and some even joined a modern dance class on campus. The school that you choose will offer many opportunities as well.

What I saw too often during law school were people who said they did not have time to exercise. They spent hour upon hour in the law library, trying to tackle the mountain of material in front of them. You could almost see them begin to wilt by early afternoon, and many of them were head-down on the desk by early evening. I think that if they had chosen to take an hour break and go move their body a bit, they would have enjoyed a much better rate of return for their study time later on in the day.

Exercise also sets good stress relief habits that will be needed throughout your career, so you may as well start the habit in law school, if you haven't set it already.

CC. ACCOMMODATIONS – RESOURCES

I didn't know where else to put this information, but thought that you would find it useful at some point. Who knows, it may save you a bundle of time and money. Good luck.

UBC – Off Campus Housing
http://www.housing.ubc.ca/other_housing/offcampus.htm;
Housing - http://www.housing.ubc.ca/

Victoria – Off Campus Housing
http://housing.uvic.ca/offcam.htm; On Campus Housing -
http://housing.uvic.ca/

Alberta – U of A Student Union Housing Registry
http://rentingspaces.ca/search.htm?ref=2; On Campus -
http://www.hfs.ualberta.ca/

Calgary – Student Union Off Campus Housing Site
http://www.su.ucalgary.ca/ooch/listing.php; Residence
Services - http://www.ucalgary.ca/residence/

Saskatchewan – USSU Housing Registry
http://www.ussudb.usask.ca/housing/default.htm; Housing &
Residence - http://explore.usask.ca/about/housing/

Manitoba – Off Campus Housing
http://www.umanitoba.ca/student/housing/off-
campus_living.htm; On Campus Housing -
http://www.umanitoba.ca/student/housing/on-
campus_living.htm

Windsor – On and Off Campus Housing
http://wilu2003.uwindsor.ca/ENGLISH/Accommodations.ht
ml

Toronto – Off Campus Housing
http://link.library.utoronto.ca/StudentHousing/index.cfm?fus
eaction=category&category=6; Student Housing Services -
http://link.library.utoronto.ca/StudentHousing/

Ottawa – Off Campus Housing
http://www.uottawa.ca/students/housing/OCH/; On
Campus Housing - http://www.uottawa.ca/students/housing/

Queen's – Apartment & Housing
http://www.queensu.ca/dsao/housing/ah1.htm

Carleton – Off Campus Housing
http://www.carleton.ca/housing/off_campus/index.html; On
Campus Living -
http://www.carleton.ca/housing/on_campus/index.html

McGill – Off Campus Housing
http://www.mcgill.ca/offcampus/; University Residences -
http://www.mcgill.ca/residences/

Dalhousie – Living Off Campus
http://www.housing.dal.ca/default.asp?mn=1.9.51; Residence
& Housing - http://www.housing.dal.ca/default.asp?mn=1.8

DD. EXAM WRITING STRATEGIES

There are some excellent resources available to help you
specifically with the art of law school exam writing. I strongly
advise you to seek out these resources as soon as possible to
gain an early advantage.

I will provide some very basic (but essential) information
here about how to increase your chances for success on a law
school exam. However, remember that none of this
information is of any use unless you have been consistent in
your readings, note taking and annotating.

Law school exams are gruelling experiences. If you thought
that the LSAT is or was a monumental challenge, wait until you
experience a law school exam. That said, there are some very
basic strategies and ideas that can help you to succeed. Before I
begin, let me just make some brief comments about law school
examinations.

First, I absolutely do not agree with the methodology used
by law schools in examining their students. 100% finals DO
NOT make better lawyers. They do not and should not act as
filters, weeding out those who will not succeed as lawyers.

What they do, however, is create a whole lot of stress, a whole lot of anonymity between law students, and create an atmosphere that does not create better lawyers. They do not emulate, in any way, real life as a lawyer.

Can you imagine a scenario like this: You are a first year associate and have been called in by a partner. He tells you that you must read the facts that have been given to him by a client in relation to a business deal that the client has been involved in which has gone sour recently. The facts are very convoluted, often unclear, and inconclusive. Unfortunately, you will not be able to access any of your notes, any textbooks, any Internet search or research tools, or any legislation. Oh, by the way, you must have a complete, coherent and legible answer, indicating all legal issues, any potential pitfalls or concerns, both for and against the client, making sure that you cite all relevant legislation, history, public policy and case law that might be pertinent. Now, you have three hours – GO!

This is just not real life people! I know that I cannot change this madness with a few paragraphs in this book, but I think that it is appropriate that I make my opinion known to you so that you can realize that you are not alone in your frustration with this system of evaluation. However, on the other side, I do realize that from an administrative standpoint, there are some arguments to be made for this type of examination, especially in law schools with larger student bodies. There are, in my opinion, many other alternatives to this scheme, but I will save those for another book or essay. Or, check out what other students are saying at www.canadalawstudent.ca/surveys.html.

The truth is, this is the methodology used in most classes by most instructors in law school. As such, we must work with it. Here are the most important considerations that you must take with you into the examination room.

a. IRAC (Issue, Ratio, Analysis, Conclusion)

Law students writing exams often overlook this strategy. Not unlike the KISS (Keep It Simple Sweetheart) principle, the IRAC principle can help you to keep your focus pointed in the right direction. Your job in most law exams is to be able to identify the key legal issues at the very minimum. If you can find more subtle legal issues, all the better. Many professors will tell you that if you can identify the relevant legal issues, half of your battle is over. Big points are given for this skill. It is not always easy to identify all of the issues that are being presented in a given fact pattern. This skill takes practice, and you should be sure to prepare beforehand by going through old exams and checking your answers with the professor or at the very least a fellow student.

The next step is to be able to provide a reason or mini-conclusion about why you think a particular issue will be treated in a particular way. Some students like to think of this step like a mini-hypothesis. Usually, you are not expected to come to a hard-line conclusion at this point. You are to identify that the issue could go in two or more directions. Identify clearly what those directions are and what the possible outcome could be.

Then comes the important part. Now it is time to put on your lawyer hat, along with your legal academic hat and hit the problem with full analytical force. Now is when you must put yourself in the lawyer's shoes, taking into account relevant legal theory, case history and legislation to fully consider the hypothetical problem you are faced with. Legal analysis proves to be the most challenging aspect of a law exam for most people. What happens too often is that the student will start down a particular thought path and get stuck on it, trying to flesh it out to the Nth degree, forgetting that other possibilities remain, only to look up from their exam paper and realize they are running out of time. In my experience, and from what my classmates have shared with me, it is much better to fully organize your analytical thoughts beforehand (perhaps in an outline form), and then to weigh the possibilities as you go along. One key aspect of analysis is to try to hook your *ratio* to a rule of law, whether it is common law, case law, statute law, or public policy. Once you have established this, your job is to find all of the possible exceptions to the rule, analyzing what might happen in the case of each exception. You may find that you have to go through this sort of analysis numerous times for each relevant legal issue.

Although not always worth the most points on a law exam, a sound and compelling conclusion can go a long way towards succeeding on the exam. Now is your chance to pound it home – your opportunity to bring it all together and come to some sort of deduction about what the best options are, in your opinion, for the hypothetical client. Remember, you are pretending that you are a lawyer. You are supposed to analyze all of the potential liabilities, risks and potential outcomes. You will want to show that you are aware of all of these, and that you can potentially identify the best scenario available and what that scenario might look like.

Law exams are very practical, pragmatic exercises for the most part. As I mentioned above, they involve a mixture of lawyerly thought mixed with scholarly theory. With the exception of a few courses that you might come across that deal heavily with legal theory, you will find that those who are able to conduct legal analysis, as when actually practicing law, will have the greatest success.

You should not limit your law exam strategy to what is written above. There are some excellent books written on the subject, including *Getting to Maybe* by Richard Michael Fischl and Jeremy Paul. This book changed the way that I approached preparation for and writing of law school exams and is considered the pre-eminent resource on the topic of law school exam writing. You can find their book at

http://www.amazon.ca/exec/obidos/ASIN/0890897603/can
adalawstud-20/701-3675836-3447539 or at http://www.canada
lawstudent.ca.

b. Don't Be Too Eloquent

A law exam is a fine balance between showing everything
that you have, and showing a mature ability to cut to the chase.
In my experience, when my writing waxed too eloquent on an
exam, I lost the most points. First, writing ad nauseam about
something that I learned over the term wastes a lot of valuable
time. Although you will be encouraged to write legibly and
cogently, there really is very little value in using expressive or
flowery language. You do not need to explain anything more
than once. You do not have to explain it in new or novel ways.
The key is to make your point, make it quickly, logically, and
well argued, and then move on. Go for the points. Get it all on
the exam booklet in a rapid-fire fashion. Then, if time permits,
go back and flesh it out, explaining more fully to show that you
have a better grasp of the material than your classmates do. It
is better to put yourself into the middle of the marking curve as
quickly as possible, and then fight for those marks that will put
you higher in the distribution. Too often, I have heard of
students who have gotten caught up on a particular legal issue,
only to run out of time before they can even identify all of the
other issues, let alone analyze them and come to a conclusion.

c. Approach Your Instructor

Again, this is key to success in preparation for an exam.
Approach your instructor about ANYTHING that you feel
you are weak on. I felt intimidated early in my law school
career about doing this. It is not easy to admit that you feel
lost. However, remember this: If you are paying $10,000 in
tuition, and you take 15 credit hours per semester, you are
paying $1,000 per course. That is approximately $25.64 per 1-

hour lecture. So, you are paying $25 per hour to be in a group session with up to 100 other students. Surely, given this very crude analysis, you deserve more for your money. I think that you can feel entitled to ask a little more time of your instructor for some one-on-one instruction on material that you feel you need help with.

d. It's All About Getting as Many Points as Possible

As I mentioned above, law school exams are a race against time. Even if you have complete mastery over one of the topics that you have covered, you cannot count on impressing the instructor by answering a single question on the exam in full essay form. You are far better served to survey the exam as quickly as possible and look for the big points and bag them. This will ensure that you get the maximum advantage out of your knowledge garnered while studying and preparing.

This can be a rather schizophrenic exercise. Many students have difficulty with organizing their writing to meet this challenge. I would suggest reading the entire exam before even setting a pen to paper. You may want to make very brief notes in the margins of the exam question paper, or on one sheet of your exam booklet. However, *force yourself to read everything once before proceeding with any answers*. It is amazing how this exercise can allow you to better see the forest through the trees. In some cases, you may even find that one question can help you to formulate an answer for another question, or trigger an idea. Also, you can see better how the marks are weighted and tackle the most valuable ones first.

Once you have read the exam, it is prudent to write a very brief outline for each question. Given your time constraints, you will want to keep these outlines to very brief language. The advantages of doing this are twofold. First, it allows you to keep everything straight while you are madly writing away on your long-form answers. Secondly, in the event where you are unable to get everything done for a question, you may be able to grab some points within the outline itself. I have often gained points for simply stating a legal issue, a ratio or a conclusion within an outline. Remember, the big points are gained for getting all the issues in the first place.

Stay organized, stay focussed, and stay calm. Those who can do these things will gain the greatest advantage. Ride the proverbial law school B curve and surf your way towards an A.

I cannot emphasize enough the importance of consistency throughout the term. Even if you use all of the exam writing strategies mentioned above, without having a good working knowledge, with focus on detail, you will limit yourself to the land of the average. Take every advantage that you can.

A Word from the Wise – Practical Experience

For exams, first I reread my class notes and then I skim at least the materials covered in the first half of the course. Once that is done, I make a condensed summary of the course, which should be no more than eight pages. This usually includes each case name, one sentence giving the principle of the case, and one or two words to remind me of the facts. It will also include a list of important definitions and the names and section numbers of any important legislation along with a one-sentence summary of each section. When this is completed, I try to commit the summary to memory, even if the exam is open book. This saves time during the exam and allows you to organize more efficiently.
— Robin Penker, University of Alberta

My typical preparation for a law school exam was to begin reviewing my notes about a month to two weeks before the exam and then to prepare my own CAN for the course. Depending on the course, preparing a CAN may take up to a week to do. I would then review my CAN and refer to any textbook for areas that I might have had difficulty with. Then I tried to answer questions on old exams to get myself into the mindset of applying the law to facts. This I usually did a couple days before the exam. The night before the exam, I continued to review old exam questions and tended to review my CAN at least twice. In some classes, I also spent time with other students in a study group to review exam questions. This is how I studied for exams all three years.

— Lorne Randa, University of Alberta

EE. 1L EVALUATION

> *Inside yourself or outside, you never have to change what you see, only the way you see it.*
> — Thaddeus Golas

You did it! You made it through your first year of law school. Exams are over; perhaps you have a week or two before you need to start your summer job. Now is a great time to look back and evaluate what contributed to your success and what did not. If you aced your exams, good for you. Make notes of what types of questions or types of issues challenged you on exams. If you achieved average grades, assess why you think this is. Remember that most of your classmates are near you on the curve. The important thing is to think of ways that you can push yourself higher on the curve next year.

Ask yourself if you need to spend more time on school and less time on extracurricular or leadership activities. Perhaps you need to change the balance of your time spent on different things. Perhaps you need to reassess working that part-time job. Avoiding debt now may have a very negative impact on your ability to make income in the future. If your grades are suffering too badly because of a part-time job, you might want to consider a higher student loan, a student line of credit, or some other means of allowing you more time to hit the books. You can pay off that money, theoretically, much faster making $30 or more an hour as a lawyer than you can at $7-8 per hour working at a café. However, do not take this to the extreme and create a situation where you have more debt than you can reasonably manage. It is just something to consider.

You may find that you wished you spent more time in study groups, more time briefing cases, more time consulting with instructors or more time conducting daily review of the material. You might want to make certain resolutions for 2L such as getting to bed at a certain time each day, or deciding to only go out one evening per weekend. You might want to reduce the time that you spend in the gym (however don't cut it out – three times per week is totally justifiable). You might want to talk to your significant other or your best friend or your family and let them know that you just cannot be quite as available in the coming year.

All of these are examples of considerations that you may want to make going into the next year. The next year will be crucial towards you gaining your articling position. You will want to find as many ways as possible to improve your chances for success. The end of the first year is the best time to do this assessment, to make strong resolutions for the following year, and then to let it rest for the next four months. Enjoy your summer experience, learn from it, and get ready for the next round.

A Word from the Wise – Practical Experience

To cope with stress in law school, I was lucky to have an understanding fiancée/wife, and a friend in another law school to talk to about common concerns.
— Shawn Davis, University of Calgary LLB/MBA

CHAPTER 5:
SUMMER JOB

The law is not so much carved in stone as it is written in water,
flowing in and out with the tide.
— Jeff Melvoin, Northern Exposure,
Crime and Punishment, 1992

A. OPTIONS

Contrary to popular belief, there are many fine options for summer employment as a law student. The following examples are certainly not exhaustive. Go into your first summer with an open mind, considering carefully how your summer experience might affect your future career choices or chances.

a. Firm

As soon as you begin your law school career, you will be inundated by both students and faculty members about the importance of working at a law firm for your first summer. You will start hearing rumours and announcements about on-campus interviews within the first month of law school. I remember coming home one day from school during first year and sharing this phenomenon with my wife. We were both dumbstruck at how quickly the fracas had begun. I had barely cracked open a textbook and I was being told to prepare my résumé and to purchase a suit for the upcoming interviews. I could not believe this for a few reasons. First, I had no idea if I wanted to work at a law firm during my spring/summer break. Secondly, I did not know if I wanted to stay in the city where I was attending law school – why would I want to jump into a firm in a city at this point without being sure? Thirdly, I didn't know a thing about law firms when I entered into law school – what was a good firm, what type of law do different firms practice, what were firms looking for in a first year law student? All of these questions swam around in my head, and I admit that I felt quite lost.

I wish that someone had taken me aside and explained to me what my options were, and provided advice towards landing a rare firm summer job. A few application deadlines went by, along with some interviews before I clued in.

A job at a law firm in pretty much any city in Canada is an exceptional opportunity. By that, I mean that these jobs are rare. You will hear repeatedly that they are imperative towards getting a good article. My experience tells me otherwise. However, it *is* a much easier way to get an article, if you happen to land one of these jobs. The number of these positions, like articling positions, declines during economic hard times. It is common to have your class fighting for 10-30 law firm jobs within the local community. That number may not be accurate, given that most major firms recruit across the country. At my school, that meant many students were left high and dry. Unfortunately, there seems to be a stigma placed on not getting a summer job at a law firm. To me, it seems ludicrous, given that the chances of landing one of these jobs is very low indeed.

Law firms come sweeping into the law schools, often sending representatives across the country, looking for the brightest and the best law students to come join them for a summer internship, with the opportunity (some go so far as to almost make a promise) of an offer for an articling position at the end of the summer employment. Many of the major law firms incorporate this recruiting technique. The argument goes that they want to get the best first – in other words, they want to scoop the competition. There is also the argument that a summer job is a great way to interview you over four months, thus giving the firm an opportunity to really find out if you are a good fit. This is a credible argument, at face value. There is another argument that this recruiting technique is an opportunity to find very cheap, very eager help. The truth is that summer interns do almost as much work, although often more menial, as articling students at a relatively low wage. This argument is also salient.

So, where does this place you? The first thing to consider is your overall intentions with law school. Do you feel driven to get the most prestigious, best paying law job available? Do you consider this the only way to justify the monstrous tuition that you are going to pay over the three years of law school? Or, on the other hand, do you want to get a better view of the landscape of the law?

These are important questions to ask, and can be answered in numerous ways. If you feel driven towards prestige, you will want to be sure to get your applications in and do your best to impress in interviews. Please read the sections on résumés and interviewing included in this book to better prepare yourself. However, remember that you are competing against the very best. The funny thing about this recruitment period is that impressions are based upon what you did during your undergraduate degree, which may have been totally unrelated to the law. It will also take into account your LSAT score. So, really, your application for a summer job is an extension of your law school application. Firms will try to predict who will be great lawyers based on these criteria, in addition to the impression that you make on them at an interview. Read the section in this book on being yourself carefully. Most of your chances are based on a first impression, as recruiters have little else to go on.

On that point, if you can find any form of contact with someone at a recruiting firm, this can be hugely advantageous to you. As with all jobs, networking is imperative and often lends itself towards success in landing a job. You will want to sweep your list of personal contacts to find anyone and everyone that works for, or knows someone who works for a recruiting firm. I know, I know – this seems like too much to think about right off the bat. I agree, but I must give you a taste of the reality of law school and your legal career.

Now, I have had many classmates who had great experiences during their summer job at a law firm. They had opportunities to be exposed to new and exciting areas of law, were exposed to the courts, honed their research and writing skills, and extended their personal network of contacts in the legal field. However, the majority of students that I have spoken to about their summer firm job have indicated that they worked very hard, wanting to impress partners and recruitment staff, that they felt a large amount of competition between themselves and other summer students, and that they felt a lot of pressure to work long hours – even weekends in some cases. All of this for around $2000 per month. Many students do express a sense of relief when that articling offer comes at the end of summer, leaving the student to relax in their upper year(s) of law school. However, I have also seen students wish that they had the opportunity to test the other waters out there, feeling trapped by a firm that has shown confidence in them. These are all things to consider in your decision to apply or accept summer firm positions.

You are not really trapped if you happen to land a summer firm job. You can always say no to an articling offer. If you feel that you have what it takes to find another article, and if you consider that this firm has shown confidence in you, you may feel that you can take a chance. However, realize that if you say yes to an articling position at the end of your summer employment, you are now bound to that agreement, and that it would be considered bad form to go back on that agreement later.

If you happen to luck out and get a job during your first summer and are not attracted to the firm, you can decline any offer and you can also try to gain employment at another firm during the second summer. However, you are now playing the odds again. That said, you do have a summer of experience to put on your résumé, and you can tell a subsequent firm that you feel you would be better suited at their firm, based on your previous summer experience.

Some firms like to hire students in their first year of studies. Others prefer second year students. There does not seem to be much logic to this. However, it seems that firms in less attractive cities (i.e. not economic centres) like to scoop students early to convince them that their firm and their city is a great place to practice, or in turn, to find students who are of this mindset already.

I did not work at a firm either of my summers. However, I had friends who did. I feel that I had better summer experiences than they did, but everyone will have their own opinion about this option.

The worst that you can do is to get your applications in early, do as much homework as you can on the specific firms, and give it a shot if you are accepted. You can always change directions later on. In any case, practical experience will make you a better student in your subsequent year(s) or will make you a better lawyer in the end.

Please note that not all firm job advertisements come out during the school year. Many pop up at smaller firms near the end of the term, or even during the summer months. There are often cases of firms looking for help on a part-time or short-term basis. Keep your eye open for these opportunities, as there might be an opening to a perfect-fit career choice for you.

A Word from the Wise – Practical Experience

Get involved in extracurricular activities. Take a hit sometimes in not doing all your readings so you can meet with firms and adequately prepare your applications.
— Shawn Davis, University of Calgary LLB/MBA

b. Internship

Many of the summer jobs that come up are internships at various organizations. These can include non-profit organizations, government agencies, advocacy groups, community foundations, international organizations, etc. There are also opportunities with various levels of courts. Postings will come up on a periodic basis. These can be excellent opportunities to expose yourself to new areas of law, to gain practical experience, and to increase your knowledge in a field that you are interested in. A summer internship can never hurt you in terms of gaining an article.

c. Corporate

Not very many law students consider this option. One of the reasons is that most corporate legal departments do not readily advertise summer internship positions. However, students, including myself, who have taken advantage of this opportunity often have great things to say about it.

As I said, most legal positions for corporate entities are not advertised. This is because they are often small departments who do not always know their budget until the last minute. Some corporations regularly hire summer students. However, even these corporations rarely advertise, but usually hire based on a recommendation or based on résumés sent to them directly by interested students.

After some consideration, I decided to apply for a position at a multi-national oil firm in Calgary for my first year summer job. This was an unadvertised position, but I did have a friend who worked at the company. I sent my résumé to the friend and asked them to pass it on to someone in the legal services department. I had to wait until almost the last minute, as the company did not know if it would be hiring until late March. I was very glad that I waited, and that things worked out.

As I said in Chapter 4, my first summer was fantastic! As I was the only summer student, I was able to receive a lot of attention from the 16 lawyers in the department. I covered about 20 areas of law, wrote many brief but worthwhile memos, and was able to attend a number of hearings, arbitrations, and conferences. I was able to meet directly with a large number of company client groups, and generally improved my legal research, writing, and advocacy skills. I was well paid compared to colleagues at summer law firm positions. Best of all, I worked a regular 9:00 to 5:00, five day a week schedule, with an hour lunch every day. Unlike at many law firms, there is no expectation of summer students, or of lawyers for that matter, to work crazy overtime hours.

During my summer, I was also able to work many hours at a local big law firm, which was partnered in a way with the corporation where I was working. This allowed me an opportunity to see what it was like to be in a firm, to see what other summer students and articling students were doing, and to get an idea of whether this option would be for me. I was able to do research in their law library, and to consult with a number of their lawyers.

Some of my classmates also took advantage of a summer position at a corporation. They also experienced a wide variety of work, relatively good pay, and relatively fewer work hours compared to classmates who were working at law firms.

When it came time to interview for articles, this experience was obviously appreciated by recruiters. It was unique and offered the recruiters an inside perspective on a major potential client. I found that they were also impressed with the knowledge I had obtained during my summer, both of the law and of corporate matters. I highly recommend this option either for your first or second summer.

d. Research for Professor

This option for summer employment is a great one. Some people look at this option as a last-resort option, but it can be an excellent opportunity to increase your knowledge of a particular area of law, can improve your research and writing abilities, and best of all, is often very flexible. These positions usually come up at the end of the school year, or the beginning of spring, so be sure to keep your eye out for them.

Many law professors are awarded research grants, part of which they can allocate to student researchers. Work can vary from researching particular legislation, case law, or historical information. It can also involve putting together casebooks for the upcoming year.

Schedules are usually accommodating, with a fixed-term contract. In other words, as long as you get the job done, you can do it however you want. Try to get an after-hours access card to the law library to allow you even more flexibility.

Many students take on research positions in conjunction with another part-time job. Research work usually pays relatively well (around $15/hour), but the hours are not always full-time.

A research position can be a great asset to you when it comes time to apply for an article. Showing that you have excellent research and writing abilities will be very attractive to an employer. As well, if you are able to improve your expertise in a particular area of law, this can also be appealing.

Be sure to be honest with your hours reporting. You absolutely do not want to tarnish your reputation within the Faculty of Law. Reporting is usually done on an honour basis. Remember, you are in training to become a lawyer. Conduct yourself accordingly.

e. Student Legal Services

This is an excellent opportunity for those of you who are interested in any type of litigation, and can be equally useful to those interested in civil matters. These positions are coveted, and competition can be stiff. If you are interested in this type of summer job, you will want to volunteer during your first year of law school. Applications for summer jobs occur early in the year. Interviewers often make their decisions based on commendations from your day leader during your first year.

There are usually opportunities on both the criminal side and the civil side. Criminal deals with summary convictions, such as traffic laws, possession of recreational drugs, etc. Civil deals with such things as small claims, landlord tenant law, family law, etc.

Working at Student Legal Services (or its equivalent) can lead to further work in your second summer as a supervisor or director.

You can expect to go to court often, especially on the criminal side, as a representative of clients or principals. You will spend a lot of time on the telephone providing information on the civil side, but may go to court as well. You will do a lot of client interviewing on both sides, and will hone your letter writing skills as well.

Articling interviewers usually look very highly upon this type of experience, as it shows that you have a high interest in a particular area of law, that you have practical experience, and that you have had a lot of exposure to clients.

B. WHAT ELSE CAN I DO WITH MY 1L SUMMER?

There's more learning than is taught in books.
— Lady Isabella Augusta Gregory

a. Study Abroad?

As mentioned earlier in this book, an international law study program may be a very good option. I had one colleague who attended the international program put on by Queen's University in England. He had a fantastic time, went on some amazing "field trips" with the program, and gained some fantastic credit towards his LL.B. By doing this, and by increasing the number of courses that he took in a couple of semesters, he was able to finish law school in 2.5 years, and was able to start his article earlier than his classmates. This is definitely a viable option. Depending on what school you attend, you may be eligible for funding for certain programs. Check with your school.

b. Get Away from Law? Travel

I have often found a tinge of jealousy in my heart towards those classmates who chose to avoid a summer law job and instead chose to embark on a travel adventure. I know of students who have gone surfing, over to Europe and down to the States. They did not learn anything about the law, and they did not increase their legal network. However, and this is why I feel some jealousy, they were able to unwind after a gruelling year of study. They were able to recover, and rejuvenate.

You might think that this option would amount to career suicide. However, from what I have heard from recruiters and from students who have travelled instead of worked during their summer, this option can be equally advantageous. However, it is important to spin your story to your advantage. Let the recruiter know why you took the summer off to vacation. Let them know that you learned a lot about yourself, about another part of the world, and about another culture (if applicable). If you travelled to a non-English country, tell them that you wanted an opportunity to improve your second or third language skills. You can also feel free to tell the recruiter that you needed an opportunity to gather energy for your all-important second year so that you could put forward your best effort to get good grades, and more importantly, to learn the law.

C. NETWORK!

Your summer job is a great opportunity to network. First, you will potentially have an opportunity to meet practicing lawyers, depending upon where you work, at your workplace. Meet as many of them as possible. Find out what kind of law they practice. Take the opportunity to share a bit about yourself, but also try to find out what their lives are like. You can learn a lot about the firm this way. It is much more revealing than the firm website! Your summer job can also be a good opportunity to meet lawyers from other firms or establishments. If you have time, take every opportunity to attend firm functions, conferences. Get your name out there!

A Word from the Wise – Practical Experience

My first summer after law school I did landscaping. I had done the same throughout most of the summers in my undergrad and knew what to expect.

My second summer of law school I worked at ATB Financial in its legal department. It was a good chance to experience aspects of the legal profession and created a number of connections for the articling process.
— Jaime Johnson – University of Alberta

D. HOW TO WRITE YOUR FIRST MEMO

Chances are that you will be asked soon after starting a summer legal position (especially at firms, corporations or another organization with a legal team) to write a legal memo or document of some kind. My first memo assignment was really quite terrifying. I was given a rather complex set of facts and was asked for a legal opinion, outlining the law, an analysis of the law, and to state a series of options available. I was given no other instruction. So, where to begin? I had only written one formal memo before this, and it was rather contrived because it did not deal with real people or a real legal problem. It had all been make-believe. But now my work seemed to count, and I wanted to get it right.

The first place to start is with the lawyer that asks you to complete the assignment. Let them know what background that you have in the area of law, ask for some clarification on the facts, the questions that are placed before you, and about what resources might be immediately available in the law library or through other lawyers in the department. That first step will be a massive help to you. Without doing that, you may be scrambling! Then go to a couple other lawyers and ask them some clarification questions and ask them where they would look first. Let them know of your background in the area, that it is your first real memo, and that you feel rather green. By doing so, the lawyers may take some pity on you, and be willing to help. You might find the response somewhat different in some firms, but I think that no sane lawyer should expect you to be an expert the first day of your first legal job! If you do get dissention or attitude, be humble, ask questions kindly, and if you do not get reasonable answers, try another source. Too often, people get intimidated, try to do everything on their own, and end up hurting themselves and disappointing the other party when they do not produce a satisfactory product.

Next, get your hands on as many textbooks and articles written on the given subject. Do a quick survey of the area of law, and try to find key words that will help you to find information. Search the online legal databases for any cases that might help shed light on the subject, and finally, do a comprehensive search online using search engines. It is surprising how much information this last step can produce. Although I personally did not use this information as my basis for analysis, it was a great tool for making me familiar with the issues and the basic law.

Once you have gathered enough information and have taught yourself at least the very basics, start to tackle each issue individually. If you can think of sub-issues, write them down and try to find answers. If you stumble on something that you need clarification on, go back and start the process over again for that issue. Finally, make yourself an outline of all of the issues, of all the relevant law that you can find, both case law and legislation, and then proceed to fill in the blanks, so to speak.

Write that first draft several times over. In retrospect, I wish I had consulted the lawyer throughout that first draft process. It would have saved considerable time on the second draft. Nevertheless, I let pride get in the way – I wanted to impress the lawyer! Again, humility goes a long way when you are a "greenie." The lawyer, in my case, reviewed my draft and had me do it again. Then again and again. I went through seven drafts altogether. At the end, the lawyer asked me what I thought of the final product. I admitted that I had not thought it would be so arduous to write the memo, but that I had learned a significant amount through the process. The lawyer said that this was a good thing, and that it would take progressively shorter times and less effort as I went along. Her prophecy was true, as each memo got much easier.

The important thing, I think, is to be sure to get help sooner rather than later, and to ask for feedback throughout the process. Many of my classmates told me stories of trying to do their research work assignments on their own, and of ending up having to redo the entire thing because they went down the wrong path. Remember, your summer job is a training opportunity, not an opportunity to show that you already know everything. Briefly, be humble and take help wherever it is given.

E. WHY AM I DOING DELIVERIES?

This was the first thing that a colleague brought up when I asked her how her summer job was going at the law firm where she was working. She couldn't believe that after completing an undergraduate degree, gaining entrance into law school, and excelling in her first year of law school, that she was being asked, on a regular basis, to deliver documents all around the city, both to courts and to individuals. She could not figure out why couriers could not be used, or why other support staff could not take care of this menial work. She was much more interested, and showed interest to her superiors, in legal research, practical application of the law to specific files, and legal questions.

I kept this thought in my mind for a couple of years, and I still do not think that I have an answer to the question. The truth is that almost every summer student (and sometimes articling students) end up having to make deliveries for stretches of time (often a day a week) during their summer employment, if they are working at a major firm. Further to this experience, summer students will often end up doing more photocopying, collating and general office work than they anticipated. There are some cases where a good principal will avoid giving you this kind of work. But, most students express that they spent much more time on these tasks than anticipated or wanted.

There are arguments that it is part of "putting in the time." It could also be a "test" to see if you are willing to do the mundane when requested (not all law is fun). There is also an argument that this is part of the practicality of being a lawyer.

These arguments do not fly with me. It seems to me that this is an opportunity to exploit eager and easily moulded individuals. Often, associates and partners are much more interested in doing other forms of legal work, are under the gun for deadlines, and the summer student seems the obvious answer to doing this menial work for them, leaving time to bill other work. On the point of billing, it is possible that your delivery is being billed to a client, perhaps at a cost to them that would boil both yours and their blood.

The reason I bring up this topic within the confines of this book is to warn you of the possibility that you may end up doing this type of work for at least part of your summer. Secondarily, it is best to avoid railing against the machine on this one. You do not want to jeopardize your chances at the firm just because you think that they are not treating you fairly and underestimating your value to the firm. Truth is, you are a summer student, and subject to the mercy of the members of the firm. They will all joke that they had to go through the same thing. Just treat this as part of the "initiation" of becoming a lawyer. A summer only lasts four months, and you will only end up doing deliveries about 10-14 times. Moreover, do not fret about doing photocopying or collating – take it with a grain of salt, and try to enjoy the downtime.

A word of warning: a number of students have shared that they wished they had been warned of the extent of deliveries and other extraneous duties. Often, students can be facing a serious deadline given to them by a partner or associate, forced to take care of these other tasks while wanting to finish an important legal memo, or contract draft, for example. Try your best to coordinate deadlines on days when you know you won't be asked to do a bunch of deliveries or photocopying. Further, let your principal know clearly what other expectations are on you and let them know that you will do your best to meet all of your duties and expectations. Many students fear looking bad, but my experience is that it is best to fully communicate your scenario and ask for help, concession, or mercy. Most principals will listen to your description and will try to accommodate you. However, be prepared for lawyers who are up against huge deadlines themselves, and who do not want to hear a thing about your problems as a summer student. Try your best to anticipate peaks in deadlines and expectations, and try to do your best to meet them early, leaving room to breath when necessary.

F. Make an impression

On the point of making impressions, I cannot say enough about the importance of this. However, making an impression does not mean brown-nosing. It means portraying yourself as a professional, or future professional. There are a number of points of advice that I would like you to think about.

Dress the part – your physical appearance does not stop being important once your interview is over. Often, students will wonder what they should wear on the first day on the job. Wear a suit. Period. The cardinal rule is that you can never dress up too much. However, you can dress down too much. Avoid embarrassment and dress up. If you find that other lawyers at your firm or establishment dress down, ask your supervisor if it would be alright if you did the same. Find out if the organization has a casual Friday, or other casual days. For casual days, do not dress down too much. Stay dressy. Imagine meeting a client – what impression would you want to leave.

In terms of working impressions, leave the very best one that you can. Meet all deadlines whenever possible. If you cannot meet a deadline, be sure to let the lawyer know as far in advance as possible. Let them clearly know why you require an extension, or if the task can be modified to meet the deadline. If you are working hard otherwise, the lawyer should make some breathing space for you. The first legal memos that you write will be extremely challenging. You will end up spending a long time on them. However, do not think that you have to do a perfect memo, without any form of blemish. No sane lawyer can expect a summer student to produce the same work as a lawyer or articling student. Do ask for feedback on your work, perhaps at stages along the way before the deadline. This is especially important for anything going to a client, as you want it to be as accurate as possible.

Much of the impression that you leave will be outside of the scope of your legal research and writing. You will likely be invited to firm functions, client functions or meetings, firm meetings, etc. These are the real opportunities to get to know the lawyers at the firm. Do your best to engage as many people as possible in meaningful conversation, showing genuine interest, while avoiding sounding too eager. When appropriate, submit your opinion on matters of interest. Treat everyone with the utmost respect, and do not be afraid to let some of your real personality shine through.

G. DO THE WORK YOU WANT TO DO

One of the most common complaints of summer students is that they ended up doing work that did not interest them. The best way to avoid this is to align yourself with partners and associates who work in your area of interest. This could mean dropping a short email to them, indicating your interest in their area of expertise. It could mean knocking on their door to say hi at the beginning of the summer, letting them know who you are and that you have an interest in their area of law. Further, you can let your principal know of your interest, and ask them if they could align you with the appropriate people. If you can do these things successfully, you should be able to fill your desk with items of interest to you. The trick is to avoid work that you do not want to do. You can feel free to let an approaching lawyer who wants to hand you some work what you are currently working on, what your current deadlines are, and whether you will be able to readily accommodate the deadline being asked for this project. However, do not become known as the summer student who says no to everything that doesn't interest them. Balance things out by accepting a reasonable amount of work from other lawyers. Remember that you are there to further develop your legal skills, and a variety of work can lead to new interests, or at bare minimum, a working understanding of a new area of law.

Do not bring your work or attitude down to that of your summer workmates. Avoid gossip. Avoid negativity. Remember, you are competing with them. Not everyone gets an articling offer at the end of his or her summer. Be sure that you do.

H. ACCEPT AN ARTICLE OFFER OR NOT?

At the end of your first summer, if you are at a firm or at an establishment that offers articles, you may have the opportunity to be offered an articling position, even after your first summer! This is a great gift for some people. For others, it can cause a very serious dilemma.

On the one hand, accepting an articling position takes a ton of pressure off you. You now can relax for your next two years knowing that you do not have to go through the application or interview process. It seems weird, I know, but these firms seem to place confidence in this early decision. They will have watched you for four months, and are willing to bet on you.

This apparent stress-free scenario can have its downfalls. For one, it can cause you to become complacent in your second and third years of study. However, the truth is that you really do have to learn the law. Some people are scared enough by the idea of showing up to the first day of their article and not being able to answer basic legal questions. Nevertheless, many others that are in this situation do become indolent and end up hurting themselves. Remember, getting the article is only the first step. You still have to impress the firm enough for them to keep you after your article, and you still have to pass the bar exam or the CPLED courses!

The other big drawback to accepting an article early in your law school career is that you are now unable to see what the rest of the market is like. A classmate of mine pined during the application and recruitment period, wishing that he could check out all of the firms that I was visiting, second-guessing the decision that he had made after his first summer. He wondered if he could have gotten a better salary, better benefits, and perhaps even a better fit somewhere else.

Some firms will try to pressure their summer students into giving them an answer right away about whether they would accept an article offer. Do not be pressured. It is a very big decision, and you are early on in your career. Very early on. Let them know that you really appreciate the offer, and the confidence that they have in you, but that you need some time to consider all of your options. Let them know what you think of their firm if it is positive, but don't sell yourself out because of a little pressure. Try to buy time if you can. Do some more research on other firms that interest you and see if you are really getting the article that you want. Chances are that if you have landed an article offer this early, you will be in good stead going into the recruitment period.

If you do accept an article, congratulate yourself, stay humble (in other words, don't brag to all your friends), and put your head down and plod forward into 2L and 3L. You still have a lot to learn about being a lawyer. Use the time wisely. You have nothing to lose now, so go for it!

I. SCHOLARSHIP APPLICATIONS

Many scholarship and bursary applications come due in May and June of each year. Be sure to keep on top of those deadlines. Do not let your hectic workload at your summer job get in the way of obtaining free money! It's a great idea to gather all of the information, contact information and deadlines into a spreadsheet and keep it with you at work and at home. I do not advise working on applications during work hours.

CHAPTER 6: SECOND YEAR (2L)

If law school is so hard to get through...
how come there are so many lawyers?
— Calvin Trillin

Second year in law school is much different for many people from the first year. Depending on the location of your law school, and what city or town you plan to article in, the second year can be the most important of your three years in law school. This is often the most important year for making an academic impression upon recruiters.

A. MARKS, MARKS, MARKS?

If there is a time to make sure you are at the upper end of the curve, it is during your second year. It is true that marks were important towards gaining a summer job in your first year, but the truth is that those positions were few. In second year, you are now in the running for a larger pool of articling positions. However, be aware that the number of positions is always less than the number of applicants. You will want to give yourself the very best chance that you can to gain the article that you want. You would much rather be in a position where you are declining article offers than having to scramble for one offer.

Nobody can predict the future, but providence favours the prepared, so prepare yourself for the battle and build up your arsenal. The best weapon you will have is your transcript, so take it seriously.

Although marks are very important in your second year, there are also some other important considerations that can provide you with a more complete résumé, excellent experience, and a whole lot of fun. I provide some examples below. Be sure to balance these activities so that you can give yourself enough time to do well on your papers and exams.

A Word from the Wise – Practical Experience

My first year marks were very important to me because I wanted to make my wife proud of me and to ensure her that we made the right decision for me to return to school. I did very well in that year, and so I have continued to put a lot of pressure on myself to keep up my marks. If one wishes to be involved in their school's law review or is interested in clerkship, good first year marks are really important.

Second years marks are definitely important in applying for articling positions. Although not the only thing a law firm will look at, they can definitely get one an interview.

Third year marks, assuming one has obtained an articling position, are not that important any more unless one wishes to pursue graduate work. I would like to keep my options open and so I still focussed a lot on getting good grades in my last year.
— Lorne Randa, University of Alberta

B. LAW REVIEW

Not all law schools have a Law Review or similar student run academic journal. If your chosen school does not, please ignore this section.

If your school does have a Law Review or other student run academic journal, you should seriously consider participating on its editorial board or committee.

In the U.S., Law Reviews are very serious business. Depending on the Canadian law school, Law Reviews can be serious business as well. In most U.S. law schools, only those who are invited get to sit on the Law Review editorial board. Only the cream of the crop ever gets the opportunity. Law Review is considered very highly by employers, and is almost always a requisite for graduate studies in law.

As an example, the Alberta Law Review, a publication that has been in print for 50 years (established in 1955, with its predecessor, the Alberta Law Quarterly, established in the 20's), follows the same basic format as the U.S. Review system. Second year students apply to the Law Review, and applications are reviewed by the Law Review executive (Co-Editors-in-Chief, Treasurer) and Faculty Advisors (usually four). Each of these people is given one vote, and out of those votes 14-16 new members of the Editorial Board are chosen. It is a big honour to be selected to the committee. Many applicants are turned down. For the most part, grades are the prime criterion for selection. However, as the Editorial Board is broken down into various committees, it is possible for a student to gain acceptance, even if their grades are not at the very top of their class, if they can offer unique and useful skills that will help the Law Review to run smoothly. The Alberta Law Review is a business with an operating budget of over $100,000. As a result, committee members are given a lot of responsibility, and it is very important to ensure that committee members have the requisite skills to complete their particular tasks. Being good at law exams does not necessarily indicate this requirement.

If you are selected to the Editorial Board (you apply in the first week of 2L), you will have a 2-year commitment, consisting of 52 hours of work per year for each of the two years for a total of 104 hours. These 104 hours are broken down into editing and committee work. Each member of the Editorial Board must complete a minimum of two full edits (usually 20-80 hours of work each) over the two years. The rest of the time is made up with committee work. As a reward for your hard work over the two years, you are given credit for one 3-credit course in the last year of your last semester. As well, as a member of the Editorial Board, you have the option of registering for the Law Review Research Paper course, which requires you to write a 20-page case comment and to present this comment to a group consisting of Editorial Board members. These two credit opportunities can really take a load of pressure off your shoulders during your last year of law school.

Other benefits of being on the Alberta Law Review include a personalized letter from the Alberta Courts inviting you to apply for clerkships with the Alberta Courts. This is a nice "in." More importantly, recruiters tend to look very highly upon experience on the Law Review. Inclusion indicates that you are most likely the best of the best, that you have gained considerable experience in legal research and writing, that you have developed an eye for detail, and that you are aware of a number of current legal issues. As well, if you are considering graduate school in law, inclusion on a Law Review will go a very long way for you, especially if you apply in the States. It is a well-kept secret that Law Review does not hold quite the same status in Canada as it does in the States.

A further opportunity comes in your third year of law school if you are elected as Editor-in-Chief (as I was). This is a full-time paid position during the spring/summer of after your second year, and a part-time paid position during your third year. This is an excellent opportunity to beef up your curriculum vitae, to make amazing contacts, and to learn leadership skills. I was able to converse often with leading academics, practitioners, and judges during my term. I also had the opportunity of having dinner with the Chief Justice of Canada, and of having dinner meetings with former members of the Supreme Court of Canada, the Court of Appeal and the Court of Queen's bench of Alberta. Among some other key things, I attribute this opportunity to landing me so many interviews and subsequent job offers during the articling recruitment period.

Each law school will have a somewhat different process and organization for their law journal. Be sure to inquire with your law school early and find out how you can become involved. Some schools will offer more or less credit than the Alberta Law Review.

C. Mooting programs

I include the major competitive moots here, but there may be more that I am not aware of within different provinces. Links to these moots may be accessed from www.canadalawstudent.ca.

The Philip C. Jessup International Law Moot
International – world's largest moot competition – more than 1500 students from more than 300 law schools in just less than 50 nations on six continents. National and international division rounds. (From U of A Website)

Kawaskhimon Aboriginal Moot
Open to all law schools – aboriginal law. Kawaskimhon means, "speaking with knowledge". The moot is typically based on a current high profile case at which Aboriginal rights are at issue.

Law Schools from across Canada represent a party or interested intervener in the case. Each team is required to prepare written factums and give oral presentations on matters arising out of the moot problem. The format of the moot is based on the traditional Aboriginal talking circle consensus building process. The Native Law Students Association of the Faculty of Law, University of Toronto held the first Aboriginal Rights Moot in 1994. Do not have to be aboriginal to participate. (From Queen's and U of A Websites)

The Laskin
The only national, bilingual moot. Open to all law schools in Canada. Usually constitutional administrative law. (From U of A Website)

Gale Cup
Sponsored by the Canadian Bar Association – Ontario – Supreme Court decision – national division and international division – open to all law schools, English and French. (From U of A Website)

Clinton J. Ford
Department of Justice of Alberta – criminal or constitutional/criminal topic – University of Alberta. (From U of A Website)

Western Canada Trial Moot
Six teams – one from each Western law school. Top three go to the **Sopinka Cup Trial Moot** in Ottawa. (From U of A Website)

Labour Arbitration Moot
Several law schools – sponsored by Mathews, Dinsdale and Clark. (From U of A Website)

Alberta Court of Appeal Moot
Criminal law, civil law (contract, property or tort law), and constitutional law – between Calgary and Edmonton. (From U

of A Website)

The Canadian Corporate/Securities Law Moot
Sponsored and administered by Toronto law firm Davies, Ward & Beck. (From U of A Website)

Niagara Moot
The Niagara Moot is an international law competition that brings together approximately 15 Canadian and American law schools from the Great Lakes region. At Queen's International Law (LAW-540) must be taken as a pre- or co-requisite. (From Queen's Website)

Wilson Moot
The Wilson Moot focuses on equality issues raised by various provisions of the Canadian Charter of Rights and Freedoms, including but not limited to section 15. This national competition is usually held in the Federal Court Building in Toronto. Ideally, students should have some background in Charter jurisprudence beyond Constitutional Law and Public Law in first year. (From Queen's Website)

Client Counselling Competition
The international Client Counselling Competition provides an opportunity for students from law schools in Canada, the United States, the United Kingdom and Australia to learn and practice interviewing and counselling skills. The competition simulates a law office interview in which teams of two students from each school interview a 'client' and are judged according to agreed criteria (e.g. ability to establish a good working relationship with clients and to develop strategies to help clients resolve their problems). Beginning with a regional competition, the winners at each level proceed to a national and ultimately an international final. (From Queen's Website)

Arnup Mock Trial

The Arnup Mock Trial is an annual competition involving two-person teams from each of the six Ontario law schools (Osgoode, Ottawa, Toronto, Western, Windsor and Queen's). This competition requires the examination and cross-examination of witnesses, submissions on motions, and opening and closing addresses to the jury. The competition usually alternates each year between civil and criminal trials. The competition is regularly held at the courthouse in Windsor and the winners go on to compete for the Sopinka Cup in Ottawa. Candidates from Queen's must have taken Evidence (LAW-320). (From Queen's Website)

British Columbia Law Schools Competitive Moot (U.B.C. / U.Vic. Moot)

The British Columbia Law Schools Competitive Moot is a moot competition between the law faculties of the University of British Columbia and the University of Victoria. The competition is held in early February at the Law Courts Building in Vancouver or Victoria, on an alternating basis. The Begbie Trophy, a sculpted trophy donated by the Superior Court Judges of British Columbia, is awarded to the winning school. (From U.B.C. Website)

ABA Negotiation Competition

The American Bar Association ("ABA") organizes a negotiation competition for law students each fall, which takes place at the regional, national and international levels. (From U.B.C. Website)

Online Mediation Competition and Online Negotiation Competition

These competitions run simultaneously: Problems are handed out in January and the moots occur in February. The mediation team, comprised of two mediation advocates and one or two mediators, will participate in two online mediations. The two-person negotiation advocacy team also participates in two negotiations. The first mediation or negotiation is "open" for one week and discussions can be synchronous or asynchronous; the second mediation or negotiation is scheduled to be 24 hours in length and may pose different challenges depending on time zones of participants. (From U.B.C. Website)

MacIntyre Cup - Western Canada Trial Competition (Sopinka Cup - Ottawa)

Open to second and third year students, annual external competition for Western Canada (first and second place teams go to Ottawa for Sopinka Cup Trial Competition). (From U of C Website)

Moncton-Ottawa Competition (French)

The Moncton-Ottawa Moot is a French language appeal proceeding on a private law issue. The two-member team is required to prepare a factum and to present its argument orally before the Supreme Court of Moncton-Ottawa. The competition is held alternatively in Moncton and Ottawa. (From Ottawa Common Law Website)

Mathews, Dinsdale & Clarke Labour Arbitration Competition

The Mathews, Dinsdale & Clarke Labour Arbitration Moot is for students who have an interest in Labour Law. The team consists of two students who must be in their second year. This moot is held in Toronto in late January. Students prepare oral argument only, but each team prepares arguments for both union and management sides. (From Ottawa Common Law Website)

Harrison Shield Moot - UNB

The school's most prestigious in-house moot is limited to third year students. (From UNB Website)

Trilateral Moot

The Trilateral Moot involves competition with UNB, University of Maine and Dalhousie University. (From UNB Website)

There are a number of internal moot competitions for upper year students at all Canadian Law Schools. Some of these competitions are qualification rounds for regional, national or international moot competitions.

D. RESEARCH FOR ARTICLES – COMPARING FIRMS

One of the biggest challenges that I faced in law school was when it came time to choose firms to send applications to. There really is a large number to choose from. It can be an arduous task to sort through all of the information.

Most information about the different firms can be gleaned from a few places. First, your career office should have some files on hand that they have gathered from various firms, outlining basic information about the firm and about their articling program. Second, Quicklaw™ now provides a lot of information on firms and articles. Lastly, and most importantly, you can gather a large amount of information from firm websites. I include government articles in this discussion.

When I first started my research, I was faced with well over 40 firms that I was considering. They were in two major cities and two smaller centres. I noticed that many of my classmates were starting to pull their hair out because they were frustrated with trying to keep all of these firms straight. Salaries, billable hours, benefits, areas of law, number of lawyers, how many articling students they accept each year, retention rates, key contact persons and many other pieces of information were swimming around. On top of that, the rumour mill started working and firm reputations often became either clearer, or muddier.

I was determined to give myself the best advantage possible. I saw one solution in creating a database of the above information. I created a Microsoft Excel® spreadsheet containing all of this information, along with firm addresses, phone numbers, key contact email addresses and fax numbers. As well, I used some basic math formulas in the spreadsheet to analyze the numbers – salaries for articling students and first year associates, and the corresponding billable hour expectations, along with vacation length and benefits. This analysis told me a lot! By laying this database out in front of me, I was able to see more clearly which firms corresponded to what I was looking for in an article, and in a potential career destination.

The numbers themselves were very revealing. I learned (for the first time – can you imagine that) what these billable hour quotes really meant. By doing some basic math, and making some standard assumptions (e.g. Using a 1.6 factor for what a billable hour equated to in real work hours), I started to get a better idea of what my life might look like working at these particular firms. I came to the insight that firms were quoting an actual workweek (using an arbitrary, but good guess of a 1.6 factor) ranging from 32.65 hours to 58.78 hours. My factor number was probably low, but it gave me a good indicator nonetheless. Further, the numbers showed me that the hourly wage using the factor above ranged from $18.83 to $28.85 per hour.

Now, these numbers may not be absolute true reflections of the real workweek hours or the real hourly wage for an associate. However, as I was analyzing the firms side by side, I think that the numbers were clearly indicative of the range of expectations and remuneration. 32.65 hours is very different from 58.78 hours! $18.83/hour is very different from $28.85/hour! This exercise was a real revelation – firms were paying drastically different remuneration to lawyers, who were, for all purposes, equal in legal experience and, potentially, ability. Worse, I had heard many rumours that a more true expectation at the higher-end firms was around 2000-2400 billable hours per year. I could not imagine a 60-hour workweek, let alone an 80+ hour workweek.

Your needs and expectations for the beginning years of your legal career may differ from mine. The point that I am making here is that a thorough analysis of the numbers, along with other criteria, can go a long ways towards making a decision that is good for you, for your partner if you have one, and for your family over the long run. The numbers were not the only criteria that I based my own decision on, but I think that I considered them a lot more closely than many of my classmates did. From my perspective, many of them based their decisions on firm reputation, how fancy the firm offices were, and in some cases, merely on the starting salary, regardless of billable expectations.

Many classmates have argued with me that in the end it all balances out – that once you are 4-6 years into your career that salaries balance out and that billable hours become more reasonable. Although that may happen to an extent (and it is my belief that the pressures at higher-end firms never really ceases), if you could avoid the high pressure and lower hourly salary in your early years, but obtain an equally rewarding practical legal education, along with similar career opportunities, why would you subject yourself to something more arduous?

My approach to the problem was that I wanted to find an article, and hopefully a subsequent associateship, at a firm that valued my time the most in the early years, that offered a solid article with a lot of support, and that valued community and family over significant profits. Your criteria might be very different from mine. You might be at a time in your life where you would not mind burning the midnight oil for a few years. I was not willing to make this sacrifice. I had come from a career before law school that demanded heavy weekly hours. I knew what it really entailed. I knew that it was not something that I wanted to subject my family to.

A spreadsheet and an analysis can also have other benefits. For one, you might come to the conclusion that you want to strive for the most prestigious, highest paying article with the possible intention of moving somewhere else later on that is more in line with your long-term career goals. I almost made that choice. Another added benefit is that the spreadsheet can make your application process go much quicker and more smoothly as you can use your spreadsheet to do mail merges for applications and for envelopes. I did this, and it saved me hours. The spreadsheet will allow you to collect all contact information in one spot so that you can easily cut and paste or a merge using Microsoft Office software. Make sure that you check and double-check all contact information in your spreadsheet. It is imperative that you get it right to avoid embarrassment and a lost application opportunity.

If you would like a copy of this spreadsheet so that you can modify it for your own needs, please send me an email at adam@canadalawstudent.ca and I will email it to you ASAP. You can fill in the information for firms that you are interested in, along with the corresponding numbers and information. If you are familiar with spreadsheets, you may like to use the "Sort" function (Data>Sort) to filter your information and sort it by billable hours, hourly wages, etc.

I also found it useful to put personal notes beside each firm. This might have included general impressions, rumours about reputation, or whatever personal criteria that might be important to you. I also used the highlight function to highlight those firms that interested me. Lastly, as I went through the application and interview process, I used the spreadsheet to track progress and results, keeping everything very organized. For example, as interview calls came in, I recorded the date, time and place of each interview. I could then easily print off the spreadsheet and bring it with me each day during interview week.

E. CAREER DAY

Career day, if your law school has one, is one of the most important days of your law school career. Absolutely, for any reason whatsoever, do not miss this event. Career day is an opportunity to meet with a large number of firms and establishments, along with some of their representatives. It is a good chance to collect brochures from each firm, to get some cool free swag, but most importantly, to mingle with potential recruiters. There are only two points of advice for this event:

1. Dress your best, and be on your best behaviour – this day, for many, is the first step of the interview process.

2. Talk to as many people as you can from these firms – this is your chance to ask questions without a lot of risk. Although you can use this chance to make a good impression, you are among a large number of other faces, and perhaps will not even be recognized at future meetings. But, more importantly, this is a fantastic free opportunity given to you to ask many questions as you would like. It is kind of like being given a "Chance" card in Monopoly – you never know what you are going to find out. You may find that gem among the candidates, or, in turn, might find out that you really do not want to work for a particular firm.

F. THE KILLER RÉSUMÉ

You can find a large number of sample cover letters and résumés on the web or in various books on the subject. I decided to include a sample of my own in this book for a couple of reasons. First, it worked for me. I am a believer that if something works once, it has a good chance of working again. You may use this sample as a template, but be sure to fill the cover letter and résumé with your own information. I include the sample here more as an example of formatting and to show what kind of content may be included. This sample may also be useful for your summer job applications or even applying to law school. Customize as necessary.

You can find other sample résumés at www.canadalaw student.ca.

I sent out my cover letter and résumé templates to a large number of classmates and professional colleagues. I also took the time to have them reviewed by our career officer at my law school. I did not take everyone's advice, as it was often conflicting. While there are different schools of thought regarding résumés, here is what I think is really important:

1. Make sure that there are absolutely no errors in these documents. A single spelling error can put your application into the reject pile extremely quickly. Law is a field of precision, and an error on your application automatically categorizes you as someone who does not take the proper care required for important documents.

2. Use the name of the person that has been indicated as the key contact person for applications. Make sure that their name is spelled exactly right. Include their position, if it is available to you.

3. Make sure that you get the address correct, on both the cover letter and the envelope. There are few things worse than having a person from an articling committee open a letter from you addressed to a competitor firm.

4. Try to fit your cover letter onto one page. I would suggest, in retrospect, that my cover letter is rather wordy. If you

are able, cut it down even more. Get the important information out as quickly as possible.

5. Try to fit your résumé onto two pages or less. This may be difficult if you have had extensive experience, both at work and volunteering. Be choosy about what you include. Put forward the best impression possible for yourself.

6. Include a list of references available as an attachment to your package. Unless requested, do not bother with copies of letter of references. Unfortunately, most recruiters do not take the time to read these. However, if reference letters are requested, ensure that these are available to the recruiter within the timeline indicated.

7. Make a personal website – it will catch a recruiter's attention, will allow them to see your pretty face, and will allow you to tell a lot more about yourself than you can on a few pieces of paper. If it piques a recruiter's interest, it may cause them to spend a lot more time on your application than on that of your competitor's.

8. Generally, do not use fancy textured or patterned paper. Stick with white.

9. Make sure everything is stapled securely together and that everything is neat and tidy (no coffee stains!).

See Appendix C for copies of the cover letters that I used for my applications, and for the résumé that I used for my applications.

a. Personal Web Site?

The best thing that I ever did related to my legal career was to create a personal website. I am convinced that this website helped me to gain acceptance to law school, to obtain numerous scholarships and bursaries, to gain summer employment, and ultimately to gain a great article.

I was lucky to have the skills to design and program my own personal website. I constructed it about six months before applying to law school. It included the following information:

1. Résumé (extended version, with links to pertinent websites, such as corporate websites)

2. Awards

3. Volunteer work

4. Accomplishments

5. Travel information and photographs

6. Volunteer information and photographs

7. Reference listings

8. Adventures and hobbies

9. Contact information

I included photographs throughout. I tried to make it very user-friendly and easy to navigate. I made the design with law firm websites in mind, trying to maintain a professional, but fun atmosphere.

I am amazed by how many interviewers, application assessors, and hiring committee members commented on my website. I included my URL address on all correspondence, cover letters, and résumés. I also carried a personal business card with my URL and email address on it. More often than not, interviewers had visited my website out of curiosity. Now that you all are advised of the advantages of a personal website, and as more of you gain the skills required to build a personal website, it may not be such a novelty. However, I still believe that it is worthwhile, as a personal website offers an opportunity for further exploration of your skills, achievements, interests and experience. It puts a face to a name, and shows some real initiative. Not everyone will be interested, but I am convinced that it cannot hurt to include a URL address with your résumé and cover letter.

It cost me nothing to build, except time. It cost me about $50 CDN a year to have hosted (go to www.doteasy.com). If you do not have the requisite skills, I suggest that you approach someone to do it for you. A personal website, such as the one that I have described above will cost you between $1000 and $2500 to have built with a professional design firm. I have built sites for other law students (I have built over 100 websites altogether in my career) and all of them have said that it paid off for them. If you think that you would benefit from a personal website, please email me at adam@canadalaw student.ca and I can either provide an estimate for you or refer you to someone who can assist you. The cost for this service will be somewhere in the range of $500. I believe that the investment in a personal website is worth it.

G. APPLYING FOR COURT CLERKSHIPS

As I did not receive a position with the courts, I asked a colleague of mine to write this section. Her experience and success is convincing:

My name is Kim Yee and as of 2005, I was a second year student at the Faculty of Law at the University of Alberta. I recently went through the process of applying for a clerkship position with the Court of Queen's Bench in Alberta, the Alberta Court of Appeal and the Supreme Court of Canada. I ultimately accepted a position with the Alberta Court of Queen's Bench commencing in 2006.

In navigating my way through the application and interview process, I learned some things that I think would be useful to students going through an experience like this. The following are some common questions that I had and I think that you may have when thinking about whether to apply for a clerkship position.

I caveat my discussion about clerkships by saying that the answers that I have provided are based on my own personal experiences and observations thus far. As of this writing, I have not yet commenced my clerkship so my opinions are derived from going through the interview experience myself, and talking with people who have completed clerkships, judges, professors, and the career services officer at the law school that I attend.

a. What is a clerkship?

The term "clerkship" can mean a variety of things. A traditional clerkship would involve working closely with one particular judge but it can also refer to a position in which the clerk serves a number of judges. The duties of a clerk include researching various points of law, preparing memoranda, writing judgments, discussing cases and case law with the judges, attending trials, hearings, etc. The type of work that is assigned to students may vary according to the court. For example, if you are clerking with a court of appeal, the assignments may differ a lot from those that you would receive in the Court of Queen's Bench in terms of length and the level of analysis required. What I think most clerkship positions share is the fact the student will have a chance to work very closely with members of the judiciary.

b. What made you decide to apply for a clerkship position?

When I was in my first year of law school, I attended an information session hosted by the Alberta courts. During the presentation, the speakers had outlined what sorts of things the students were able to participate in while clerking, what sorts of skills they wanted to foster and what former clerks had gone on to do in their legal careers. After hearing the presentation, I knew that this was something that I wanted to do. If your law school offers a presentation such as this I would highly recommend attending, even if at first blush you don't think that this would be something that you would want to do. I certainly did not think, when I entered law school, that this was something I would want to pursue, but once I learned what it was all about, I was convinced that this would be a fantastic opportunity and a great fit with my personality and interests.

c. What are the benefits of a clerkship?

There are so many. The following is a list of the main benefits:

- The opportunity to participate and observe how the justice system works from a very unique perspective;
- The opportunity to get to know the judges and other staff at the court house that you may be appearing in front of or working with in the years to come;
- Exposure to a range of different practice areas (this is really beneficial if you are not sure what type of law you may want to practice in the future);
- An opportunity to see what sorts of things judges consider to be important when analyzing the law or the facts of cases;
- The chance to hone your research and analytical skills (this will serve you well, especially if you want to go on to do any graduate work in the future);

- The opportunity to see the law in practice;
- The chance to see a variety of different written and oral advocacy styles; and
- Most future employers will see a clerkship as an asset.

d. Are there any drawbacks to doing a clerkship?

I think there are very few drawbacks and the benefits heavily outweigh the potential setbacks. In talking with people that had completed clerkships, I heard very few negatives about their time at the courts. One drawback that I have heard about is the fact that doing a clerkship as part of an article may actually extend the length of your article. In Alberta, for example, if you article with the courts, your term there will be ten months, but you must also complete a five-month article with a firm. This is a three-month difference from those who simply article with a firm for twelve months before their call to the bar. For many others and myself this is not a major drawback at all.

I have also heard from students that a potential downside to clerking with the courts is that when they do finally arrive at the firm that they will be articling with, they feel "behind" as compared to the other articling students, at first. One person that I spoke to said that even though he felt this way he said it was very temporary; and on the upside, he had more experience than the other articling students in other areas, especially with procedural matters.

e. What does the application process involve?

This will vary slightly from province to province and with the level of court that you apply to. However, generally the courts will want the following:

- A cover letter stating why you are seeking a clerkship position

- A current résumé
- Current transcripts (of all post-secondary marks)
- Letters of reference (including an academic letter of reference from a professor)
- Possibly, a short writing sample such as a case comment or an essay.

Each court will have a different deadline for applications. Be careful not to miss the deadlines, as they are often many months in advance of when your position will commence. For example, for me, the deadline for the Alberta Courts was in December of 2004 but the position will not commence until June of 2006.

Once I applied, I heard back within a couple of weeks. In most instances, I was notified by e-mail that I had gotten an interview.

In determining which courts to apply to, I did some research about what sorts of work the different levels of court did and what sorts of experiences former students had with the different courts. The sorts of cases and the type of work that clerks do will vary widely from court to court.

f. What is the interview process like and how can students prepare?

I interviewed with the Court of Appeal in both Edmonton and Calgary, the Court of Queen's Bench in Edmonton, and the Supreme Court of Canada. All of my interviews were very different, but the one thing that I think that they all shared was the fact that, at the end of the day, the judges were really just trying to get a sense of the applicant's personality. As a result, the questions were geared towards that end.

For the Alberta courts, the process was very much the same – the courts appointed a justice or two to conduct the interviews for the entire court. In all of my interviews, legal counsel to the court played a large role in the interview and selection process. They were also present during the interview and asked questions of the applicants as well. The interviews lasted for about twenty to thirty minutes.

The Supreme Court of Canada was quite a different experience from the Alberta Courts. I applied to the court as a whole but each justice chooses whom he or she would like to interview. Theoretically, one could have nine different interviews. Some justices will want to talk about the law and others will ask the applicant questions about themselves or you may get a combination of both sorts of questions. The interviews have a strict time limit of thirty minutes, which goes by very quickly. Unlike with the other courts I interviewed with, legal counsel did not sit in on the interviews.

In general, I found that the appellate courts tended to ask more questions about where my legal interests were and what sorts of research and writing skills I possessed. There was definitely more of an emphasis on these skills and academic ability.

In terms of preparation, I would suggest approaching it the same way you would any other job interview. You want to emphasize the attributes that you possess that they are looking for. For the courts, this would be research, writing, communication, interpersonal and analytical skills. The most important thing is to relax and be yourself. I know that it sounds trite, but once you have an interview, you are generally in pretty good stead. The justices are now trying to get a sense of who you are and what you would be like to work with on a daily basis. The interview process can be quite intimidating, but I think that there are things that you can do to make it less unnerving, such as being well prepared in terms of knowing your attributes, what sorts of work the court does and knowing a bit about the judge interviewing you. Knowing some recent case law from the particular court is an asset as well, especially if you are interviewing with an appellate court.

g. How important are marks?

I think that they are important, but they are generally less important than applicants think they are. A certain level of academic achievement is required to get you in the door, but not all students that are chosen for clerkships are "Dean's list" students. Additionally, if marks were the be all and end all, then the courts would not need to conduct interviews at all. They would just take the top applicants that applied. Research and writing skills are important, so if you are not on the Dean's list but you have research and writing experience, such as being on the editorial board of a law review, experience doing research for faculty or employer's, or involvement with large writing projects in your legal or undergraduate studies, these are things that you should definitely emphasize in your résumé and cover letter, as well as in your interview.

Also, if you have anything in your background that is particularly interesting, mention it in your résumé, even if it is not an academic attribute or even remotely related to law. One lawyer that clerked with the Supreme Court shared with me that the majority of applicants have the academic ability to do the job in the judge's opinion. So what determines whether an interview is granted or not is whether you stand out from the other applicants in some other way. If you do get an interview, something interesting in your résumé will often be a topic for conversation between you and the judge.

My advice would be to strive to get the best marks possible, especially in your research and writing courses, if you are thinking you may want to do a clerkship. However, do not disregard the idea of applying if you find that you are not at the top of your class. After all, there is nothing to lose by applying. You may be pleasantly surprised and get an interview.

h. What other things can students do to increase their chances of getting a clerkship position?

- I would recommend getting involved with both law related and non-law related extracurricular activities. The courts (and other potential employers) are looking for well-rounded students.

- Get to know a few of your professors quite well, especially those who will have an opportunity to see your writing. This will make it easier for them to write a good letter of reference, should you need it. They also have their own insights about the clerking experience that they are usually happy to share with students.

- If you are interested in clerking, talk to fellow students in upper years that have gone through the experience of interviewing with the court that you are interested in.

- If your law school hosts an information session, attend, and try to introduce yourself to the judges, legal counsel, and clerks that are in attendance. These will likely be the people who will be choosing who will get interviews and who will ultimately get clerkships.

- Apply for a position on the Law Review if your school has one. This is a great chance to gain exposure to legal writing and I know that the courts pay a lot of attention to this on a résumé. That being said, this is not the be all and end all either, as I know people who were not on the Law Review who got a position with the courts.

- Get as much experience as you can interviewing. Some schools offer workshops or similar things to help students prepare. I think this is a great idea and will only help you to feel more at ease if you do get an interview with a judge.

i. Does a clerkship have to be done as part of an article?

This will vary from province to province and from court to court. I know that in Alberta you must be an articling student to apply, as the program that they have in place is an "articling program." However, the Supreme Court of Canada will take applicants who have completed their articles and who have been called to the bar.

j. Are costs covered for an interview at the Supreme Court of Canada?

My travel costs, i.e. flights, meals and taxis, were covered when I travelled to Ottawa.

k. How important is it to speak both English and French for the Supreme Court of Canada?

Being bilingual is definitely an asset when applying for a clerkship position at the Supreme Court of Canada. While I was there, I observed a lot of conversations in French between the clerks, justices and support staff. However, I did talk to someone who had clerked there and did not speak any French at all. She said that it was not a problem and that there are positions available for those who are not bilingual.

l. What kind of hours do you work with a clerkship?

From what I hear, the hours are a bit shorter at the courts than they would be at a firm and weekends are not required. At the information session I attended, the justices said that on occasion, if they need something done right away, a student may have to stay late, but that is not the norm.

A Word from the Wise – Practical Experience

My worst interview experience was with the Federal Court of Canada. I knew very little about what to expect and our career advisor in the Faculty provided little help. I had three interviews with judges - two in person and one over the phone. Two out of three went well, despite not expecting substantive

law questions in the interview. The worst interview involved a question asking me what three Supreme Court of Canada decisions did I think influenced the law the most. I was not expecting such a question, went completely blank, and could not think of any case names. It was quite embarrassing.
— Lorne Randa, University of Alberta

H. APPLYING FOR 2L SUMMER JOB

The process for applying for second year summer jobs is really the same as for first year summer jobs. Be sure that you are aware of all deadlines, do as much networking as possible, and consider all possibilities that were mentioned earlier in this book.

CHAPTER 7: SECOND SUMMER

English Law prohibits a man from marrying his mother-in-law.
This is our idea of useless legislation.
— Shawn Davis, University of Calgary LLB/MBA

A. WHAT SUMMER JOB IS BEST?

You will want to do your research in advance regarding which summer is the best to apply for in your chosen city. Some cities have a trend of hiring summer students in their first year of law school. The reasoning behind this trend, from what I can tell, is that these firms are looking for a level of loyalty. They are interested in applicants who show a genuine interest in articling and practicing in their city. Hiring early also helps these firms to plan for the next two years. Remember, a summer job at a firm is really an extended interview. It allows the firm to consider you carefully for a potential articling position.

Other cities have a trend of only hiring second year summer students. The reasoning behind this trend is that these firms are more interested in hiring applicants that are more experienced. As a result, these students will often end up with responsibilities that are more substantial.

B. ARTICLE APPLICATION PROCESS

a. Timing

For most of you, this will be the pre-eminent experience of your law school career, and the one that you will want to concentrate the most attention towards. Regardless of your grades in your first two years or how many extracurricular activities you have been involved in, you can succeed during the recruitment period. However, there are some important – key, in fact – considerations that you must address during the two months surrounding recruitment.

For many students, the timing for the article application process is abysmal. For one, you may be busy with a summer job. For another, you may be out of town (surfing, perhaps?). Lastly, you are probably tired, or even burned out from your second year of law school. I hate to break the news to you, but too bad. Now is the time to turn on the after-booster and really get to work.

So, clear your schedule as much as possible. Talk to your summer supervisor. Most firms will allow for some time to accommodate the recruitment period. Let your boss know well in advance what recruitment will entail for you – when they should expect you to be missing from work, and how much time you will be spending on arranging appointments.

A Word from the Wise – Practical Experience

To gain an articling position I would advise other students to make as many professional connections as possible. It is not that a connection will lead to a job, but it likely will lead to an interview, which can be the biggest hurdle. Meeting and impressing others already in the profession will allow for your

face to be remembered when an application shows up in the future.
— Jamie Johnson, University of Alberta

b. Application Packages

Many of my classmates have indicated that they wished they had prepared their application packages before May came around. In fact, they wished that they had prepared their packages in March, before exam preparation. This is good advice. At the very least, you should have your résumé and most of your reference letters prepared and available. It may be difficult to get reference letters from professors you have during 2L second semester, and these may have to wait until the last minute. You are also well advised to prepare a template cover letter in advance.

It is up to you to submit a full package. Be sure to read very carefully the application instructions for each firm or establishment. Follow them to the tee! Do not make an omission and risk potential rejection at the point of opening your application.

Keep your application material neat and clean. Do not do your preparation work while drinking coffee or eating breakfast. Everything must look perfect and professional. You may consider using a conservative font, and conservative paper, envelopes, etc.

If possible, prepare a thorough spreadsheet or database of potential articling employers. If you would like a copy of such a template, please email me at adam@canadalawstudent.ca and I will send you a free copy for your use. This can keep things organized, but can also save time if you know how to use mail merge on your word processor.

c. Multiple Cities?

Many people wonder and ask whether they should apply to firms in more than one city. In the U.S., it is a given that most students apply for jobs post law school in more than one city, often in more than one state. That is the nature of the legal profession there. Here, in Canada, things tend to be more localized. Although it is definitely possible to gain employment in a city other than the one where your law school is located, the percentage is relatively low. Firms tend to put a lot of emphasis on where you are from, what connections that you have to a particular city, etc. They are making a serious investment in you as an articling student, and it is in their best interest to hire people who will be loyal. It is part of the due diligence process to find out where you are from, where your family or friends live, and what your plans are.

I applied for jobs in three cities and one town. I had not yet decided where I wanted to settle down with my family. There were very attractive firms in areas of Alberta. I felt that I needed to go see first hand what the firms in all of these places were like before I could count them out. It ended up causing a lot of work and travel for me, but I do not regret the decision to apply to multiple places. Had I restricted my applications to the city where I graduated, I would have always asked "What if...?" As it was, I ended up going to the city that was initially last on my list. Why? Because I loved the firm, what they stood for, and I loved the idea of bringing my kids up in a smaller community. Do not limit your possibilities just because of the potential for some inconvenience over a couple of weeks.

That said, you should be very careful during the recruitment process – especially during interviews – to perhaps keep your cards close to your chest, so to speak. If, by chance, you are called on the fact that you have applied to more than one city (the legal community is surprising small, and this happens more often that you would imagine), do not be intimidated by the fact that the recruiter has found this out. Be forthright with them – let them know that you were merely looking into the possibility of another firm, but that you would love to stay in or go to the city that you are currently interviewing in (assuming this is not a lie – don't lie!), and that you are basing your decision more upon the firm rather than the location. If applicable, point out again the connection or nexus that you have with the relevant location of the firm you are interviewing with. In other words, make this a non-issue to the best of your ability. Sometimes, it will be a make-or-break for the recruiter, but if that is the way it goes, there is not really much you can do about it. So, do not sweat it.

d. Hidden Rural Gems

I was unsure if I should include this section in this book, as I believe it is one of the best-kept secrets out there in the Canadian legal world. Please forgive me for my bias. I realize that there are many options available to law students, and it is ultimately up to you to decide what is best for you. Some of you may want to skip past this section – those of you who love the fast pace, the excitement, and the fun of the big city. Those of you either who are repelled by these things, or who seek after a more balanced, relaxed, family-oriented atmosphere, please read on.

There are numerous opportunities to both article and practice in small to mid-sized non-metropolis firms, and at sole practitioner offices. They are not as plentiful as big city firms, and do not advertise for articles very often, but they offer a legitimate opportunity to practice law in a more relaxed rural-based centre.

A firm outside of a major centre may offer many advantages to the up-and-coming lawyer. First, are the expectations placed upon both articling students and young associates. While billable hour expectations are stated between 1500 to 2400 at big city firms, you might find 1000 to 1500, or in many cases, no billable hour requirements at all in a small town or small city firm. What does this mean? Let me provide an example. If I was comparing a big city firm who indicated a 1700 billable hour goal, this would equate to 34 billable hours per week, based on a two-week annual holiday. The small city firm who expected 1000 billable hours would equate to 20 billable hours, again based on a two-week annual holiday. 14 hours a week sounds like very few hours, doesn't it. But, a billable hour is, on average, more like 1.5 to 2.4 hours of actual work, as you will often have administrative, networking, business development, and other distractions. Using a 1.6 factor, the big city firm would equate to 54.4 actual work hours. Using the same factor of 1.6, the small city firm would equate to 32 actual work hours. That is a difference of 22.4 working hours per week. Imagine what you could do with an extra 22.4 hours per week.

A more realistic comparison would be to look at a firm that had an expectation of 2000 billable hours per week. The reason for this is that although you may be told that there is a billable hour expectation of 1500 or 1700 or 1800, the actual expectation, due to very high competition amongst associates and a bonus structure, may be much higher than that. You may get a higher expectation than the 1000 billable hours, for example, at the small city firm, but even so, you will only ever be as high as the very lowest billable hour expectation at the big city firm. So, for fun, let's do a comparison between 2000 big city billable hours and 1200 small city billable hours. The actual work hours (at 1.6 factor, two weeks of holidays) will be 64 and 38.4 hours respectively. That is a difference of 25.6 hours. That is a lot of extra free time!

My comparisons are not scientific, by any means. However, they start to open your mind to the actual ramifications of high billable hour expectations that you will inevitably find at big city firms. The truth is that my numbers are probably pretty low, regarding the factor rate, and real life billable hour goals and competition. This is why you hear of lawyers working 80 to 100 hours per week. An 80-hour week is equivalent to 11.43

hours per day, seven days a week! Or, you can take it easy on weekends, and only work five hours each on Saturday and Sunday, or crunch it all in on Saturday and work ten hours. This will leave you with a mere 14 hours a day during the week. Not bad, eh? It seems preposterous, but this does happen!

I like to look at this problem in terms of hourly pay rates as well. Some people think this is a petty way to look at things. They are career people, and the money is not the important thing. Or, the money will come later, when they make partner. This may ring of truth. Nevertheless, consider this: Let us take a 60-hour work week (pretty common at top-10 firms in major centres). As of 2005, an average first year associate position in Calgary, Alberta is paid an estimated $65,000 annual salary. You will work around 3000 real work hours during the year. Working 60 hours per week, that will give you an hourly rate of $21.67. If you work 80 hours per week, you will make $16.25 per hour. I know of quite a few non-professional jobs where you can make this much money per hour, and you have evenings and weekends off. Something to consider. Now, if you were at a small centre firm, where you worked 1200 billable hours, you would actually work around 1920 hours in a year. I will provide a salary of $45,000 (an estimated firm first year associate salary). This puts you at an hourly rate of $23.44. It is not a smashing hourly rate, but it certainly beats $16.25 and is better even than the $21.67 an hour quoted above for the big firm. At the big firm, you only get paid $20,000 more a year, but you end up having to work so much more. Another great thing about small centres is that cost of living is usually much lower. Houses go for much less than in big cities! I plan to explore other moneymaking opportunities with my spare time. What do you plan to do with your spare time?

I mentioned that some small centre firms do not have a billable hour scheme. These firms will often comment on how they can still thrive with everyone working a 9-5-type schedule. Time will have to be put in when an important case or file requires it, but on the whole partners and associates, and even some articling students, will express that they spend most weekends and evenings at home or with their family.

It boggles my mind that most graduating law students go into their article and their associateship without really thinking about the ramifications of the billable hour scheme at the firm they have chosen. Classmates and colleagues seem to shrug their shoulders and say that is just the way it is. Although it is my personal opinion, I believe that is not just the way it is. This scheme is a product of huge mergers and of well-tenured partners who need to keep fuelling the partner profit pool. In order to do that, they must keep bringing in, and turning over, if necessary, young and relatively cheap associates. Your work will be billed out at a much higher rate than what you are paid. You are cheap labour. Don't kid yourself. (Ouch! I apologize if this hurts, but it really is the truth).

Don't get me wrong. I realize that you might not get all of the same experiences at a small centre firm as you would in a big city. You probably will not get as many high profile cases, or the fancy corporate files. However, you will probably get a more hands-on experience, with more access to clients and to the court system. This does not turn everyone on. If you are not excited about meeting clients or going to court, do not worry. It is not requisite for a small centre lawyer to do these things.

A colleague of mine recently made a very astute comment while we were running together. He mentioned that when considering the whole billable hour thing, it probably makes a big difference if you have a family. I asked him what he meant. He told me that for youthful law graduates who are often relatively inexperienced with the working world, the high expectations are not as daunting as maybe they should be. A person with a spouse or partner, or more significantly, children, or a person who has worked in a high pressure, high hours job before law school will have a great advantage in understanding what high billable hours can really mean. He said that when you have children, you have a better understanding of how difficult it can be to accommodate your children's needs. You can appreciate better any spare time, such as the spare time indicated in my examples above.

A high billable hour scheme can often trap a young person who is planning to have a family some time in the future. Imagine the 24-year-old law graduate. He gets his article at a top-10 firm. He is happily and regularly putting in 12-14 hour days. He decides to buy a new house and a new car – he is making good money – why shouldn't he? Then, he finds his dream girl and marries her. The wedding is expensive, but he puts it on credit – he is going to be rolling in money as soon as he hits partner. He starts wishing he could spend more time with his spouse, but both of them appreciate the good money that is coming in. Besides, they decide that they want to start a family, and there are some expenses that come with that. They buy a bigger house, a minivan to augment their car. The children start coming. Children bring a whole bunch of potential expenses with them.

So, now our young lawyer has children. A couple of years go by. He starts really wishing that he had more time to spend with them. But, now he is totally trapped. He wants to make partner. Once he makes partner, he can really start making good money, and hopefully start working a little less.

The truth is, in my opinion, all of this can be avoided if you seriously consider what you are getting into right at the beginning. You may not like the idea of a smaller centre, or a smaller firm. But, start thinking about the future, about what you want your life outside of the office to look like. Even 100 less billable hours a year can make a huge difference. At the 1.6 factor, 100 billable hours is 160 actual work hours per year, which is equivalent to 3.2 hours per week (factoring in a two week holiday). You can be spending those 3.2 hours per week with a spouse or a partner, or with your precious children.

I am passionate about this topic. The reason is that I have three wonderful children whom I love to be around. I want as much free time as possible. As well, I worked very heavy hours in business before entering law school. I had a good understanding of what a 60 or 70 or 80-hour work week felt like. I was always wishing I could have more time with my spouse. Because of these things, I chose to article in a small centre. Again, I realize that I have a definite bias, and that these factors do not relate to all of you. You will have to make your own decisions based on your own values.

We had a presentation at my law school on small centre articles and firms during my second year of law school. At that presentation, some math was discussed that really raised my eyebrows. I will use the Alberta statistics, as the presentation was by Alberta lawyers. I think that the concepts will transfer to almost any province.

According to a presenter at my law school who worked in a small city, the Canadian Bar Association (CBA) conducted a study about six or seven years ago (the CBA could not find a copy for me before publication of this writing). In this study, the CBA tried to come up with the most optimal number of lawyers, compared to a city's population, so that every lawyer could make a good living. The optimal number that they came up with was about one lawyer per approximately 1200 people (1:1200). The ratio in Edmonton at the time of this presentation was about one lawyer per 550 people (1:550)! In Calgary, the rate was 1:450! I was astounded. This could not be right! Then, the presenters gave the ratios for small cities in Alberta. In Red Dear, the ratio, including the metropolitan area is around 1:2400. Lethbridge has a similar number.

What do these numbers mean? It means that there are many more lawyers in big cities, and that it is more difficult for everyone to have a decent piece of the pie. It also means that perhaps there are not enough lawyers in smaller centres. With law school graduation numbers staying the same, or in some cases, increasing year to year, it seems to me that more graduates should be looking to smaller centres to establish a living.

Consider these ideas, both for smaller centres, and for smaller firms within big centres. Prudent consideration early on can save you literally thousands of hours of work. You will have been in school for a long, long time. You deserve a little free time, don't you?

e. Match Program

Depending on the city where you will be applying for an article, the match program may apply to you. Be sure to ask your career officer for a full explanation of how this system works, as it can be rather complicated. It is a system that is meant to make things fair for the students and the firms, but there can be problems for those who do not follow a simple path. Do not feel that you must only apply to match program firms.

You can find a good description of the match program at http://www.commonlaw.uottawa.ca/eng/student_services/car eer/handbook/ch9_articling.htm#a9.

The Alberta Matching Program is described in full at http://www.natmatch.com.

If you are juggling match firm interviews with non-match, be aware that you must get out of the match before you accept any offers from a non-match firm. This is difficult but one can receive comfort from the fact that you can be open with the firms about your interest and they can tell you if you are in their top ranks. They cannot ask you to tell them how they rank with you, but they can reassure you of your standing with them.

f. Scheduling Interviews

One of the most common comments made by articling applicants is that they have not left enough time between interviews. This is especially true for students who are applying to more than one city.

What type and how many interviews will depend on the city that you are applying in, and what firm you are applying to. You should count on your first interview at a firm to take at least an hour. Some only take 20 minutes, but make sure that you leave a lot of time, just in case. You will find that some firms use the first interview as a quick filtering system, getting rid of undesirable applicants promptly. Other firms will try to consolidate their time and efforts, and make the first interview the only interview. It is hard to predict what format a firm will follow.

Another common comment made by applicants is that they did not make sufficient time to accommodate second interviews. You should account for a second interview for every firm that you apply to. As such, you should try to reasonably crunch in as many first interviews early on in your recruitment schedule. With second interviews, you should schedule up to two hours, minimum. Again, some second interviews can last only 20 minutes – it might be a situation of simply getting a second opinion from a second or third interviewer. Some can last a long time, can include a lunch, supper, or drinks. Third interviews are rare, but can happen, so be prepared for them.

If you decide to apply to multiple cities, you may find great difficulty in scheduling interviews that fit perfectly into your plans. Some firms will want to bunch their interviews into certain times of the recruiting week, and will not accommodate you easily. Try, if you can, to schedule all interviews in your second choice city on one particular date. Also, try to leave one day open at the end of your recruitment week to accommodate second interviews in that city. This is difficult because you do not know who will actually call you back until they do call. It is hard to be logical when you may feel uncertain or even desperate. You need to prioritize and even gamble a bit.

I applied to firms in two major cities. I personally found it to be a nightmare to schedule. I ended up having to drive to the second city directly after one interview to attend a supper interview, and then having to drive back at 11:00 pm, arriving home around 2:00 am! Then, I had to get up for another interview for 8:00 am. I was not very fresh at either of those interviews, and wished that I had scheduled things differently. I ended up having to drive back and forth four times. I would not recommend trying to apply to multiple cities, unless the recruitment week is distinct in each city. You may feel like you are improving your odds, but I think that you may be putting yourself at a disadvantage because of being drowsy and unfocussed in your interviews.

Because of scheduling conflicts, fatigue, or deciding that they have found the firm of your dreams, students will sometimes feel that they should cancel an interview later on in the recruitment week. Do not feel bad about doing this. However, do it with tact. Some firms will take it personally and will not treat you nicely for cancelling on them. This may be especially true if you cancel on a second interview. However, you can have an attitude that recruitment week is for you more than it is for the firm. There are plenty of qualified applicants out there who can fill the position. There may only be two or three firms that fit your bill. When you call (do not email to cancel!), ask to speak to the interviewer(s) directly. If they are not available, leave a message with their assistant. Let them know why you are cancelling. In some cases, a firm may call you back to try to reschedule if you are encountering scheduling difficulties – especially if the firm is interested in you. If you have already chosen the firm(s) of your dreams, the recruiters will probably appreciate knowing as soon as possible that you are out of the running for them. I do not advise mentioning why you do not want to work for the particular firm you are cancelling on. It simply does not achieve anything for either you or the firm. Just politely cancel and move on.

g. Phone Message

It is a very good idea to make sure that your voice mail or answering machine message sounds professional and cheerful, includes information about how you can be contacted (i.e. cell phone number), and perhaps indicates when you will be able to return messages (i.e. by the end of the day, or within 24 hours). It should include your full name (first and last) as well.

If you live with roommates, parents, siblings, spouse or partner, advise them of how you would like the telephone to be answered. Let them clearly know how important it is for them to sound cheerful, professional, and serious. I have heard nightmare stories about mothers talking to recruiters about their sons and daughters, or of a roommate answering the phone with a burp. Promise to take housemates of concern out for drinks or dinner if they will just behave for the next couple of weeks. It is very important. Also, advise them to take good notes when receiving a message. Supply a message pad, and multiple pens right beside the telephone. If possible, have them forward messages to your cell phone immediately so that you can reply as quickly as possible.

h. Cell Phone?

I found a cell phone to be an indispensable device during the recruiting period. It allowed me to receive telephone calls from recruiters immediately, or to return messages as quickly as possible. It can be useful to only include your cell phone number on your résumé if you would like to answer all calls directly and avoid the housemate issue mentioned above.

A cell phone also came in very handy when offers were being made. It meant that I was not pinned to my landline all day long. Offers will often come in later in the day, when first choice, or second choice candidates decline offers. There is a good chance you will be third or fourth, and you want to be available to take that precious call when it comes.

If you do not use a cell phone very much, like myself, you may want to consider purchasing an inexpensive phone and purchasing a pay-as-you-go card. Top up your phone with enough to last for the recruiting period. If you run out of time, you can simply purchase a bit more time. This way, you are not locked into a contract that you may not need later on.

There are some rules about cell phone use. Make sure that it is deactivated (i.e. silent) whenever you are going into an interview. There is almost nothing worse than disrupting an interview with an irritating telephone ring. You will cause embarrassment both for yourself, and for the recruiter. It is highly unprofessional! Also, do not take calls when you are on a loud train, or going under a light rail transit tunnel. It will sound bad on the other end.

Set up your voice mail according to the message rules above. Answer all calls professionally and cheerfully, indicating your full name. Even if it is a secretary calling you, you want to sound as professional and cheerful as possible. They may pass on their impression to a recruiter. It is best to play it safe.

i. What to Wear

There is only one rule about what to wear to an interview. You cannot overdress. This is one of the most important events of your life, short of your wedding, the birth of a child, or something like that. As such, put in the effort to look your best.

Make an investment in a decent to good suit. You will end up using the suit when you article, so it is probably a good investment. Do not buy a cheap suit. Borrow money if you have to, but do not go to your interviews looking anything but sharp. You will want to choose a conservative colour. However, there is no specific rule about having to wear a grey, black or blue suit. Wear a colour that is attractive on you, and which you are comfortable with. Make sure it fits well, and you will be set. For the record, do not wear khakis, sport jackets, or anything that is not a business suit. You will show up to your interview rather embarrassed, and will immediately stick out negatively. This is not an opinion – it is a rule. Also, buy good shoes. People do notice shoes (I had seven interviewers look me up and down – all the way to my shoes). Shine your shoes – do not let them get dirty. Good shoes are also very good as you will put on quite a few miles during interview week, and it will save a lot of pain. Break shoes in before interview week if you can.

For men, buy a few good dress shirts and have them pressed before interview week. You will have to change a number of times, both due to perspiration, and so that you can potentially avoid wearing the same thing to two interviews at the same firm. There is a debate about whether you should wear a white shirt or jump into colours or patterns. It is my opinion that it does not really matter. Just make sure that your shirt is contemporary, subtle, and attractive. I wore subtle coloured pattern shirts to all of my interviews. Purchase a few attractive ties. Try to match colour to your personality. If you are a fun person, choose a fun pattern and colours. However, do not go too loud. You may want to match patterns and colours with the firm you are interviewing at. A tie that is darker than your shirt looks best. If you can, coordinate your tie with your shirt and your suit. If you know that it is a conservative firm, wear a conservative tie. If you know it is more forward looking, hip, and young, wear a corresponding tie. I kept a few ties that were pre-tied in my attaché case and switched if I needed to between interviews. You should probably avoid bow ties, bolo ties, or anything of the sort. Save that for when you are well established at the firm. You can find out more about choosing ties, tying ties, and more at www.tie-a-tie.net.

Men should avoid jewellery, other than watches, wedding rings, class rings, engineering rings, or some other subtle ring. Earrings should really be avoided, even if you are trying to make a statement about your personal agency. You may have a belief that you would not want to work at a firm that would judge you for wearing an earring. However, remember that you probably will not be working directly with the interviewers once you are hired. In my opinion, such a subject is better addressed once you have started the job. You may want to keep an eye out when you are touring the firm for men that are wearing earrings. If this is important to you, you can get a feel for what others are wearing. Things are a lot more liberal these days, but why eliminate yourself from the running for a great article because of a jewellery statement? A good dress watch can really set your suit off. Cuff links are even a possibility, if it suits your personal style. Again, you cannot overdress.

You may want to invest in a good attaché case. It helps you to look professional, provides a space to put your résumé, cover letters, map, cell phone, snacks, etc. However, be prepared to be teased by fellow classmates that you meet on the street. It is very easy to spot articling applicants by their fancy suits, shiny shoes and shiny attaché cases. Do not be affected. You want to look polished, professional, and on top of your game.

Get a good haircut about a week in advance of articling week. Do not gamble on a hairstyle that is far off from your regular look. Depending on the type of firm you are applying to, you may want to look for a more conservative look. However, I am aware of students that have been hired with long hair, spiky hair, etc. I am in no position to suggest personal style to you. However, the general rule is that you do not want to give an interviewer any reason not to hire you. On the flip side, an interviewer may appreciate that you have contemporary style, including your haircut, especially if the interviewer is relatively young herself.

You might want to avoid facial hair, unless it is your regular style. A subtle beard, goatee or moustache may be acceptable, but I would recommend going to an interview shaved. You may want to avoid contemporary styles such as "soul patches," "razor blade" side burns, and things like that. Again, it sets you apart as not taking the interview seriously.

There is a lot of controversy about what women should wear to an interview. I am not a fashion consultant, but I do have some strong opinions about this controversy. Wear what you want to wear. If you want to wear a skirt with your suit, wear one. If you do not, do not. In this case, unlike the earring issue above, you do not want to work for a firm that will judge you based on the bottom half of your suit. The earring issue is more of a professional standard issue. The skirt issue is discrimination. Again, this is only my opinion. A number of my classmates have expressed that they chose to wear a skirt to avoid elimination from any potential firms. Again, it is up to you.

Women should follow the same general advice written above for the men. Avoid perfume, or keep it to a very bare minimum as a courtesy to your interviewers who have to stay all day in one room. That is, unless you have found perfume to be to your advantage in the past.

Women should also have a few blouses available to change. You may be able to mix and match your suits as well to achieve a different look for multiple interviews at a single firm. Again, perspiration can be a problem solved by having multiple shirts. Jewellery should also be kept minimal and rather conservative. Avoid multiple earrings in each ear. Avoid facial piercing. Again, do not provide any reason for rejection.

Do not take any of this advice personally. It is for your benefit. It is not a rejection of your personal style, or an attempt to bolster the already too-stuffy and too-conservative atmosphere of the legal community. It is advice given to provide the best possible chances for you to obtain that coveted articling position. You might want to prove me wrong. Go ahead if you want to. However, you will be fighting the odds, and I do not see why you would want to make an already challenging experience tougher on yourself. Law is a professional career. Conservative attire comes with the territory. There is more relaxation today compared to even five or ten years ago, but interviews are the time to look your very best. Wouldn't you rather be in a position of turning down offers than scrambling to get even one offer? This is the truth of the situation, and I recommend that you give yourself the very best chances.

These rules and this advice apply equally to formal and informal interview situations. Even if a partner invites you to lunch, or out for coffee, do not think of removing your tie, or dressing down in any way. Even if it is casual Friday at the particular firm, do not give in to the temptation to follow suit and dress down. Not even for after-hours receptions or drinks. You are always being scrutinized. The interview never stops until you are in your car, or on the train or bus, going to your next interview or home. Again, you can never overdress for an interview.

If you have experiences contradicting or supporting my advice, please share them at the www.CanadaLawStudent.ca website.

j. Interviewing

Interviewing is an art. There is no right or wrong way to conduct yourself. However, a few tips are worth mentioning.

First, you should attempt to be as professional and as courteous as possible. This includes basic manners such as please and thank you, and holding the door for others, and waiting for the person(s) on the other side of the boardroom table to seat themselves first. It also includes avoiding gum chewing, distracting mannerisms, putting your legs up on the table, and so on. Really, this is common sense, or at least it would seem to be common sense.

Law interviews tend to be very laid back (except for government, from my experience). They will often take on a conversational tone. Welcome this tone. However, do not become so relaxed that you start coming across as unprofessional. Avoid vulgar language, or off-colour jokes. Steer clear of putting others down, even if the other side goes this way. Maintain integrity and composure at all times.

It is a great idea to move the focus towards the firm and the interviewers if you have the opportunity. Once you see a gap in the conversation, feel free to ask questions about the firm and about the interviewers. People love to talk about themselves. However, do not forget to tell about your and your experience. Take the conversation as it comes, and remain confident.

It is a good idea to avoid interrupting an interviewer. Let them have their time to share with you. You will often be able to pick up on key points, such as what the firm is looking for, what areas of law are important to the firm, and so on. However, if you feel that the interview is being monopolized by the interviewer(s) (this is a common problem), feel free to interject at an appropriate time and either ask a question, or offer some useful information about yourself.

The interview will often extend beyond the boardroom. You may have the opportunity to tour the firm with a current articling student. You may be introduced to associates, partners and support staff. Use this time wisely. Do not let your guard down. But remember that you are interviewing the firm at the same time and use these opportunities to get a sense of the culture and tone of the firm. Current articling students may give you a sense of the reality of the firm better than the wining and dining partners.

You are being assessed during this time just as much as you were in the interview room. Lawyers, apparently, will often ask articling students and support staff, as well as other associates and partners, about what their thoughts on you are. This same stuff applies to dinners, luncheons and wine and cheese events that you are invited to.

The bottom line is: be on your best behaviour, come across as relaxed, and let your true self (at least your better self) shine through.

If you face a difficult question, or a compromising question, do not lose it. Take a few moments, take a breath, and think about how you should respond. If it was an inappropriate question, feel free to let the interviewer know that you feel it was unsuitable and why. If the matter is pushed, let them know that you will not answer that type of question. If you are wondering what types of questions I am talking about, imagine being asked if you are married or have kids, if you are gay, if you drink, if you are part of a political organization, etc. These have no bearing on your ability to fill the role you are interviewing for, and should not be tolerated. If the interviewer insists, you might just want to shut the interview down. You do not want to work at that type of firm anyway.

If you think that you have bombed an interview, do not fret. I thought that I bombed a particular interview and ended up landing an offer from that establishment. I never would have thought that would happen. But, it turns out that the interviewers appreciated my honesty and forthrightness. Never say die!

A Word from the Wise – Practical Experience

My first interview [for a summer position] was by far the worst but only because I was very nervous and I thought it went really badly. That said, two years later, when I was interviewing for an articling position at that same firm they said they remembered me from that first interview, were impressed, and that was why they wanted to see me again. Even the worst interviews might not actually be so bad.
— Robin Penker, University of Alberta

At one particular firm, I was about half way through an interview and it seemed we were really just having a hard time making conversation. At that point the interviewee stated that "sometimes you have to sacrifice your family for your career." I immediately determined that this wasn't the firm for me. To finish off the interview I was asked if I had any questions for the firm. My mind went completely blank on anything that I had read about the firm and I couldn't come up with a single question.
— Jaime Johnson, University of Alberta

k. Be Yourself

For me, this was the most frustrating and confusing mantra reported by fellow students, former students, career advisors, and networking contacts. What does it really mean to "be yourself," and does this advice really carry any weight?

Does "be yourself" mean that you should recite a poem if you are a poet? Does it mean that you should talk about hockey if you are a die-hard hockey fan? Does it mean that you should be exuberant if you are a born extrovert? Does it mean that you should tell jokes, or show your wit if you are a person of humour?

This mantra makes a lot more sense to me post-articling week. Law interviews are a very funny thing. With only a few exceptions, my interviews were extremely casual affairs. There was very little to no discussion of the law. Discussion ranged from current affairs, to sports, to my children, to my travels, to my ancestral background, to my networking contacts, to my personal business experience, and to a mountain biking accident I had had a few years previous (I included photographs on my personal website. There were references and questions about law school experiences. In my case, about particular professors, particular classes and their usefulness, the Law Review, extracurricular activities related to law school, etc. The exceptions to this rule were with government-related articles, where substantive legal questions were asked. These were not difficult questions, and were easily prepared for.

As the articling week progressed, I realized increasingly that interviewers already knew a whole lot about me before I even entered the interview room. They had read my résumé rather carefully, had perused my website (sometimes to a greater extent than I thought they should), and in some cases had spoken to other people about me. As well, some of them had already contacted references that I had provided. Wherever possible, I had also asked networking contacts to put in a good word for me. So, there was really no reason to try to impress by pretense.

The interview is really an opportunity to get a "feel" for each other. You will hear quite often that interviewers are looking for a good "fit." This rings very true, in my experience. You are also best served by trying to look for a good "fit." What is a good fit? This is where things become very subjective. For me, a good fit was a family focus, with a large range of potential legal practice areas. I was also looking for relatively low billable hours and many hands-on solicitation and litigation opportunities. I wanted a smaller firm size, with few articling student positions, so that I could get the attention that I deserved as a Student-at-Law. I was also looking for genuine sincerity in my interviewers. For you, criteria might include good humour, a more mature atmosphere, a more young and energetic atmosphere, a quick partnership track, lots of social events, etc.

I would like to provide a caveat for the "good fit" idea. For the most part, law firms are identical. Most of them run on the same billable hour scheme, have more male partners and associates than females, are profit-focussed, have annual ski trips, family picnics, associate retreats, benefits, article rotations, etc. It is hard to find firms that have a unique way of doing things. You will find more distinctiveness in smaller firms, as they tend not to be quite as profit-focussed, and are willing to look outside of the big-firm box. My caveat includes the fact that most law firms are identical in many ways, but also includes the fact that interviewers are not always a true reflection of the firm that you are interviewing at. As a result, you are best served to meet as many people as possible at the firm that you are interviewing at. If you are offered the opportunity to meet with current articling students, jump at the opportunity. These students are as close as you will get to the truth within the walls of the firm. They are not far removed from where you are, and will often be quite candid about certain things, such as what their real work schedule are like. They will also provide some of the ins and outs regarding certain associates or partners that are great or terrible to work with. If you have the opportunity to meet with partners or associates, also jump at the opportunity. Time spent doing this can pay off immensely down the road. If you can, sit down with these people face to face in a closed office. People tend to be more truthful behind closed doors.

So, what does "be yourself" mean? It means all kinds of things. I have told you some things to expect at your interview. The rest is really up to you. Be relaxed. Be confident that the interviewer is genuinely interested in you. You will have already made it through a huge cut. Often firms will receive upwards of 100-150 or more applications. Most of them only make time to interview 30 or less applicants. This means that you are high up on their radar screens. My theory is that once you have made it into their doors, you are on equal ground with the rest of the interviewees. Now is your time to shine. Now is your time to impress upon everyone that you meet that you will be a fantastic person to work with, to play with, and to show off at firm meetings and most importantly to clients. However, do not feel that you need to come across as something that you are not. Put in the time to get a good number of interviews, and then just relax.

A Word from the Wise – Practical Experience

Once you get an interview, I think the most important thing in gaining an article is to at least appear self-confident. Even if you feel like you are in way over your head or are under-qualified, walk into the interview as though you belong there: smile, shake hands, speak clearly and in a conversational tone. If the interviewers see that you feel confident about your abilities, they will be more likely to think that you actually do have the abilities they are looking for.
— Robin Penker, University of Alberta

Be the kind of person the interviewers would want to have dinner with. Be pleasant, appropriately humorous and give the appearance of being driven ... be relaxed. The idea is that everybody should be comfortable in their own skin.
— Rob Nelson, Queen's University, University of Calgary transfer student

This means being comfortable and acting as you would around friends and family. This also means being proud of who you are and what you have accomplished - but don't brag or be cocky. However, one must ensure they are still being professional.
— Lorne Randa, University of Alberta

You don't want to come off as "affected." However, you have to go into interviews with a sense of confidence in yourself. As well, you want to present yourself as someone that your interviewer could see working side by side with.
— Mike Kariya, University of Calgary

I think that [being yourself] means to just let the your personality come through in the interview so the interviewer(s) can get a sense of who you are in a short period of time. The firms will be interviewing a large number of very good students and I think that personality is what sets people apart.
— Kim Yee, University of Alberta

Don't talk about scholastic achievements. You are smart enough to work at the firm otherwise you would not have gotten the interview. Talk about extracurricular interests, travels, and know a little about the city/school of the interviewer(s). Don't be a boring schmuck who the interviewer would dread meeting in the copy room of the firm late on a Thursday night.
— Shawn Davis, University of Calgary LLB/MBA

1. Prepare

Practice, practice, practice. I wish I had practiced more. I had a willing audience in my wife and some fellow classmates, but I was too proud to take them up on their offers. I think that it would have helped me greatly, especially in my early interviews. I ended up using my first 2-3 interviews as practice, and finally started to relax. Had I practiced beforehand, I might have put myself in a better position for my early interviews.

Know your résumé and cover letter inside and out. Know the dates, know the names of all referees, employers, professors, etc. Generally, do not include something in your application that you are not intimately familiar with. There is nothing worse than being asked a question about your résumé that you cannot remember details about. It is embarrassing, and really tarnishes your trustworthiness. If you have an opportunity, review your cover letter the night before, or at the very least, right before the interview occurs. If you have dropped a name in your application, make sure you remember their name, their position, and their connection to you.

Know where you are going. Double and triple check your addresses before articling week. Write them down in multiple locations on your person (i.e. keep a copy in your attaché case, your suit, and perhaps on your Palm Pilot or Planner). I used MapQuest™ (www.mapquest.ca) to create and print out maps for any firms where I was unsure of the location. This helped immensely to save time while travelling from one interview to the other.

Call to confirm times, addresses, and names of interviewers if you are at all unsure. Be very polite when you are doing this, and let the person who you are talking to know that you simply want to ensure that you do not miss this very important meeting.

Review the firm website. This is imperative. Review the websites of firms that you are interested in very well. Read the interviewer bios, if you know whom the interviewers are. Read about what areas of law that the firm practices. Read the articling student section. Read up on firm clients, firm managing partners, firm history, and anything else you can find to give you an edge.

m. Ask the Right Questions

After reviewing the firm website carefully, prepare a set of questions that are specific to the firm. Add these to your general questions that you will have prepared before interview week begins.

What are the right kinds of questions? This is definitely a subjective thing, and I cannot tell you what exact types of questions to ask, as your needs and desires will be individual. However, you should consider the following types of questions:

- *Can you give me an example of a case that you are working on?* Ask this question of partners, associates, and especially current articling students.

- *What did you do last weekend?* This will reveal how much the person works on weekends, and will reveal what kind of outside interests the person has, providing a potential opportunity to find a common interest.

- *What kind of feedback do you provide to articling students?*

- *How often do your Students-at-Law go to court?*

There are many other great questions that you can ask. Be creative.

n. Reveal Intentions

One of the most common mistakes made by articling applicants is to be afraid of revealing their intentions. There is a general feeling that things should be held close to their chests, and that they should not reveal anything, thus giving them the upper hand. In my experience, the exact opposite is true. When you do not make it blatantly obvious that you are very interested in articling at a given firm, you make the decision much more difficult for the interviewer. If it is between yourself and another person, they will usually go with the person who shows the most interest.

This is a tricky area, because you may want to avoid any kind of dishonesty. If you think that you would rather work at two or three other firms better than you would like to work at this particular firm, then you will have to frame your comments carefully. You may want to say something like "If I were to receive an offer from you, I would be very excited about the upcoming articling year." You will be telling the truth, assuming that you only received an offer from this firm. Any offer is better than no offer. If you think that the firm is in your top 3, tell them that they are in your top 3. Tell them that you would be thrilled if you were given an offer. It is better to turn someone down once they have given you an offer than to take yourself out of the running by holding your emotions to yourself.

In my case, I received an offer from every firm where I expressed something like what I have written above. In two other cases, I know that I was in the top three or four positions, but because I didn't come across as being absolutely excited about a potential offer, I did not receive an official offer. In my case, that was OK, because I was sure that I would receive offers from some other firms that I liked better. However, if you are feeling like your chances are not as high as you would like, you will want to be sure to extend an impression, as honestly as possible, that you would be delighted to work at that particular firm.

You will also help yourself if you blatantly tell the interviewers that you intend to make your home or keep your home in the city where the firm is located. Provide as many connections and reasons for living there. I think that you cannot hurt yourself, and will probably help yourself immensely by expressing this. Of course, nothing is written in stone, but you want to show a real intention. If you are honest with yourself, you *will* have a real intention to live and practice where you are applying.

If you will be clerking with a court, be sure that you express this, and let the firm know what you intend to do – that you plan to complete your clerkship as quickly as possible, and return as an associate at the given firm.

A Word from the Wise – Practical Experience

I picked a firm that would be a good springboard in case things did not work out. At the same time, I chose a firm that I thought would provide me with fantastic articling experience.
— Rob Nelson, Queen's University, University of Calgary transfer student

---

o. Try to be Honest

The section above expresses that you should frame comments as honestly as possible. I cannot emphasize the importance of honesty enough. On a personal basis, I really believe in honesty and integrity, but that is not why I advise you to frame your comments truthfully. The reason that I implore you to remain as honest as possible is because the legal world is an incredibly small world. It is common to have articling committee members from distinct firms that are friends or colleagues outside of the office. Remember – they were potentially classmates not so long ago. I have heard of committee members from different firms getting together to talk about candidates, or even talking on the phone about potential candidates. You absolutely do not want any discrepancies coming across. This will immediately take you out of the running at both firms. This may sound paranoid, but it has happened. You would not want it to happen to you.

Besides this reasoning, it is better to be honest, and end up at a firm that suits your needs, concerns and desires than to try to pretend to be someone that you are not, in the cause of getting a job. If you work hard enough in your preparation, you should be able to rest on your qualifications, your interview skills, and your personality to get that job of your dreams.

p. Bow Out When Appropriate

If you find that you would not fit in at a particular firm, or if you feel confident that you will be able to get a better offer at a firm that is better for you, please contact that firm as soon as possible. You are in a great position, and should not feel the need to block up a spot at that firm. Remember your poor classmates who are not so qualified as you. They are desperately trying to get a job. This is also the classy thing to do, in terms of the firm. They will appreciate your polite decline to a second interview, or to an offer. This will make their job easier. Be sure to let them know why if you can. Do not tell them that you think their firm sucks. Let them know that you have found a firm where you believe there is a good fit, or that you are interested in practicing in an area that is not offered by their firm, or that you have decided to move to another city.

q. The Thank You Letter

This is essential. It is difficult to fit in, timewise, especially if you have a very hectic interview week. However, it is so important. Many applicants overlook this practice, and I think that it hurts many of them. A thank you note is a great opportunity to get your name in front of the interviewers again, especially after a day of mind-numbing interviews. It is also an opportunity to express how well you thought the interview went, how there is a great fit between the firm and you, why you think you are the perfect person for the job, and why you would be thrilled to accept an offer from the given firm. Again, use honesty when framing your note.

The note itself can take a few forms, depending on your personal style, the time that you have available, and what you think the interviewer(s) would be most comfortable with. I have used emails directly to the interviewers. It is important that you get your note to the interviewer as soon as possible, hopefully within the same day of the interview. You may want to send another quick email at the end of recruiting week. Another method is to send a letter or card through the mail, but this can be slow. My favourite technique is to keep a stack of small subtle and professional looking thank you cards with me at all times. If I was able, I would either sit in the foyer for a couple of minutes, and give the card to the receptionist, or if I was jumping from interview to interview, I would take a few minutes writing the cards, and then quickly swing by the firms where I had interviewed to drop off the card. You may think that this is overdoing it. I do not. You will make a great impression, and the interviewer will probably appreciate the personal touch. As well, a handwritten card will likely get the interviewer's attention much better than an email. Lawyers get up to hundreds of emails every day, and are especially hard pressed to go through all of them during interview week. A nice personal card delivered to their desk or mailbox will definitely stand out more than an email. Another technique is to leave a voicemail message. This can be equally as effective as a handwritten card. However, be sure to rehearse what you will say, or use the rerecord function if you are not happy with your first try. Come across as professional sounding as possible, and as sincere as possible, but don't overdo it.

I re-emphasize the importance of the second thank-you message at the end of the interview week. This is a great time to remind the interviewer of your keen interest. This will immediately put you ahead of other candidates.

r. Call-Back Interviews

The majority of firms will conduct a second interview for those candidates who interest them. If you get a callback, congratulations. You are now in the top tier of applicants, and your odds have increased dramatically. Now is the time to really turn on the charm, and convince the firm that you are the person for the job. These interviews can differ in style from firm to firm. In some cases, a second, third or fourth interviewer will interview you – perhaps the other members of the hiring committee. It may be a more formal interview, or a more casual interview, depending on the firm, and on the interviewers. A partner may interview you or partners, who will have the final say, may conduct the interview. You may be taken on a tour of sorts, briefly meeting a number of associates and partners. Some will even have you sit down individually with associates or partners. I understand that this is less common in Canada, as compared to the U.S. You may be invited to a lunch, a supper, or out for coffee or drinks. Some invitations end up in group situations where several candidates are invited to dinner or cocktails together. Remember, in any of these situations, you are being interviewed. Unless you are expressly told to take down your guard (i.e. to take off your tie or remove your shoes) you should be cautious about your conduct. Be sure to schedule plenty of time for these second, or in some cases, third interviews.

s. The Witching Hour

The witching hour is that hour between 8:00 and 9:00 a.m. on a particular set out day where firms can begin making offers. This is the time when applicants are anxious, perched by their phones, praying for that elusive offer. It is a very nerve-racking time, and a very important time. Again, this is a VERY IMPORTANT TIME. Do not schedule anything during this time. Stay close to your telephone or cell phone. You do not want to miss an important call and risk losing any opportunity.

It is very important to be realistically considering options ahead of time and to prepare to have a choice. Choose a wise friend to talk to during this stressful time for advice, perspective and stress-relief.

t. Accepting an Offer

So, you received an offer. Congratulations! You are now in a position of great power. If you have received more than one, you have even more power. However, you must treat that power appropriately and ensure that you get off on the right foot with your future employer.

Some students get excited when they receive their first offer. They often accept right away. I would advise against this. As I said, you are in a position of power. It is a good idea to let this idea rest with you for a while. It is also a good idea to see what other offers come your way. You may be pleasantly surprised. Even if you were not on the top of the list at other firms, as offers go out, and as students reject those offers because they want to go somewhere else, the firms go down their list of candidates until they find a successful match. Therefore, do not be too anxious to accept an offer on the spot.

The appropriate way to buy yourself some time is to express that you are very flattered and excited about being offered articles at the firm. Let the recruiter know that you are very seriously considering their offer, but would like to think about it, discuss it with your family, etc. Let them know, clearly, when you will get back to them (they will usually want to hear back within 24 hours). You may want to ask further questions of them, or ask for another tour of the firm and an opportunity to meet more members of the firm to help you make your decision.

Once you have done this, you can now sit back and revel in the fact that you now have an article. Do the same with other incoming offers. Take time to consider all of your options. Sit down and figure out what is important to you. Is it money? Is it more free time? Consider carefully the salary and billable hour expectations. Consider the amount of holiday time offered, benefits offered, what kind of office you will have, etc. If you have offers from more than one city or town, sit down and do a pro-con assessment of living in each centre. Use these 24 hours wisely and you will end up in a situation that is best for you.

Once you have decided which offer you will accept, you may want to phone the firm and ask some more questions about the offer. You can ask whether salary is negotiable, or whether any other point is negotiable. Some firms will not budge. However, some firms are open to negotiation. Do not worry about offending the recruiter or the firm. It is your right to ask these questions. Remember, they expressed that they want you to work for them. Now, they need to convince you that they are the best firm for you, and that they will meet your interests. Going through this process can have great financial benefits, and can provide you with a sense of control going into your article and into your career.

Do not demand more money, benefits, etc. Remember, it is a negotiation. Also, do not tell the firm that you are balancing their offer with another firm, and that the highest bidder wins. Use tact and be courteous. Maintain a professional relationship through this period and it will pay dividends once your article begins.

Now, some of you will be very happy to accept an offer right away from your number one choice. That is your prerogative. However, you may want to adopt the strategies above before you do this to increase your satisfaction with your choice. If you are afraid of stepping on toes, don't be. It is your right to ask questions, to negotiate and to make an informed decision.

C. SCHOLARSHIP APPLICATIONS

In the midst of all of this excitement during your 2L summer, it is important to avoid missing important scholarship and bursary application deadlines. Along with this, you should obtain letters of reference well in advance, hopefully near the beginning of your break from school. Once you have received your grades, you can approach professors and instructors that you did well with, or with whom you have established a good relationship. I have seen quite a few students slap their forehead during June, July and August because they were too caught up with work and articling applications and neglected to submit a scholarship or bursary application. This is too costly a mistake to make!

CHAPTER 8: THIRD YEAR (3L)

If Moses had gone to Harvard Law School and spent three years
working on the Hill, he would have written the
Ten Commandments with three exceptions and a saving clause.
— Charles Morgan

A. WHAT CLASSES?

Choosing classes in your last year of law school can be somewhat tricky, or it can be as easy as you want to make it. There are two ways to go about it.

The first is to contact the firm that you will be articling with and ask them if they would recommend any courses for you, based on what area they think you might fit in best. Be careful with this approach, because you may be pigeonholing yourself too soon. However, some firms may want you to take particular courses such as Trusts or Sale of Goods or Taxation, for example, just to get a good rounded familiarity with particular areas of law. You may be able to figure this out for yourself based on what you know about what areas of law the firm practices in.

The other approach, and the one that I agree with most, is to take courses that you find interesting or that you think you might like to practice in one day (even if it is far in the distance). Secondly, I believe that you should not try to kill yourself in your last year. In my case, I was beat by my last 2L semester. I wanted courses that would catch my attention on a daily basis. I was attracted by more practical courses, as they interested me more than theoretical ones. You might be the opposite. Although it was recommended by some "experts" that I should take certain courses to prepare me for the bar exam / CPLED courses, I did not take that advice. I figured I would learn that material when it came time. The truth is that most law students will have some major gaps going into their articling year. It is simply not possible to cover everything.

Thus, I recommend having as much fun as possible in your last year. Consider the professor/instructor teaching the course. By now, you will have picked some favourites. Consider class size. It might be more or less fun to be in a smaller class, depending on your preference.

Some people really sweat over this topic. I say let them sweat. You will have more fun, will be less burned out going into your article, and will enjoy better long-term health.

A Word from the Wise – Practical Experience

I chose upper year courses based mainly on two things. First I looked for ones that interested me but would still add possible value to my future career. Second, I listened to suggestions from articling interviews and upper year students.
— Jamie Johnson, University of Alberta

I took classes that I was interested in, regardless if I would practice law in that area or not. If you take classes that you enjoy, you will learn more and do better. But I would also recommend taking at least a couple courses that are typical areas a lawyer may face such as wills or estates, land titles or real estate transactions, judgment enforcement or personal property security, trusts and bankruptcy. These classes will help one become well rounded in the various areas of law.
— Lorne Randa, University of Alberta

B. Moots?

Moots are a fantastic opportunity to gain some practical advocacy, research and litigation experience. If you have any leaning towards litigation, negotiation, or other alternative dispute resolution mechanism (mediation, arbitration, etc.), a moot in your last year can do wonders for increasing your knowledge and confidence. It is also a fantastic way to boost your GPA, as moot coaches/instructors tend to give pretty high marks, as the rules about grading curves do not usually apply to registered moots.

Moots are hard, intensive work. However, you can learn more in a moot than in most classes. Further, most moots do not take a whole semester to complete, including research, writing and oral practices, thus freeing up time and energy for your other courses.

C. Pass/Fail courses

Pass/fail courses are a great option in your third year. They are also great in your second year. However, I think they are best done in the last year. By this time, most of you should not be too worried about your GPA, unless you do not yet have an article, or if you are considering legal graduate work. If you are in these situations, a pass/fail course is still a great option, as it will not affect your GPA. Your average will be based on your remaining courses.

Pass/fail courses tend to be a little more laid back. The pressure of the grading curve is gone, and you can use your energy to actually learn the practical aspects of the given course. Be warned, however: pass/fail courses often involve role-play exercises of some kind.

D. RESEARCH PAPERS?

Research papers, for some students, are the best thing since sliced bread. Many law schools offer the option of conducting independent research and writing a major paper on the subject. There is usually no corresponding scheduled lecture. As such, you are free to manage your own time, to pursue an area of law that has struck a chord with you, and to practice your legal research and writing abilities. You will have to obtain a faculty supervisor for your research and paper. This person will provide a certain level of guidance, including suggestions for topics, analysis of your paper outline, and will ultimately assign a grade to your paper. Most professors take on four to six independent research papers per year. Grades tend to be on the higher side for these papers. This may correspond with a relatively better quality of research and writing. In turn, it may correspond with the low number of people on the "grading curve." In any case, it can be to your advantage.

The important thing with independent research papers is to begin your research as early as possible. It is easy to become lazy and to procrastinate. Many students hammer out their research and writing at the beginning of a semester. This can be a great advantage to you both for reducing stress during your semester, and when exam time comes along.

Many lecture-based courses include a major paper as the main or only method of evaluation. These can be wonderful experiences, especially if the course subject interests you. Some professors will assign a participation mark, but some will not. In any case, it is not difficult to skip classes if you so desire, without much chance of repercussion. If you are getting burned out, either in second or third year, a paper-based course can be a real relief.

It may surprise you, once you enter a paper-based seminar, how many of your classmates will be diligently taking notes. It is my personal opinion, shared by a select few, that this is a complete waste of time. I personally hated taking notes all throughout school, as I found it to be a real distraction to actually learning the material discussed in class. I also found it very tiresome to concentrate on transcribing a lecture for 50 to 75 minutes straight, sometimes for two or three classes in a row. Unless you are aiming to create a personal library of notes to refer to when you are bored during your article year, it is not necessary to take notes during paper-based lectures. The exception is when your paper topic is being discussed, or when a particular item comes up that you think might relate to your paper topic in some way. Otherwise, I believe that you should sit back, listen intently, and relax. This is a great opportunity to engage in discussion, to practice your oral advocacy skills, and to actively analyze a particular area of the law, and to formulate personal opinions about the law.

I know some students who choose to skip most of the lectures and to work on their paper during that scheduled time. Be careful about this plan, as most people have difficulty adhering to a self-imposed schedule like this. For some people, I suppose, feeling obligated to go to a lecture can be motivating. I tend to tune out more often than not in this style of lecture. It is not my fault. I am a visual, tactile learner, and lectures have never worked for me. I would much rather read a book, or formulate a fancy spreadsheet with all of the legal concepts involved all right in front of me. I like to draw diagrams that help me to "connect the dots" as well.

Be careful not to take too many paper-based courses. It may seem like a dream to have fewer lectures and fewer exams, but papers can be very demanding in their own right. As well, avoid these classes if you have any sort of motivation challenges, as nobody will be putting the gun to you to be prepared on a daily basis, or to work on your paper regularly.

A Word from the Wise – Practical Experience

I much prefer papers. Papers give you the ability to learn an area of the law that you are interested in and provide a depth of study that exam based courses do not. Also, paper-based courses give you greater control over your grade. An exam, on an off day, can kill your grade but a grade on a paper is more directly related to the work you put into the paper.
— Robin Penker, University of Alberta

I prefer papers because there is less chance that you will miss a key issue after having conducted considerable research.
— Shawn Davis, University of Calgary LLB/MBA

I preferred courses with exams over courses with papers because I found that paper-based courses had twice the workload for the same amount of credit. This is because with paper-based classes the student is assigned readings each class, plus they often have to prepare for a presentation on top of research for their paper. For an exam-based course, the workload is focused just on the curriculum and does not require any additional research and work. However, if one is required to write a paper during their degree, like at the U of A, I would recommend taking an independent research course (especially if they are dedicated and can self-motivate).
— Lorne Randa, University of Alberta

E. WHAT TO DO IF YOU DIDN'T GET AN ARTICLE (YET)

Learn the art of patience. Apply discipline to your thoughts when they become anxious over the outcome of a goal. Impatience breeds anxiety, fear, discouragement and failure. Patience creates confidence, decisiveness and a rational outlook, which eventually leads to success.
— Brian Adams

Depending on the year that you graduate law school, and depending on what city you originally apply to article in, you may find yourself amongst a group of students who enter third year without obtaining an article position. This realization should not be accompanied with any sense of shame. This does happen. There are limited spots available in the mainstay law firms and organizations. The truth is that law schools churn out more graduates than the system can currently handle. So, where does this leave you? There is no "best answer" to this problem. However, I do have some words of advice that may help you.

First, it is time to regroup. Go back to your 2L assessment. Do you need to seek some help from a mentor, or from a book or two, in order to improve your GPA? If so, get right on that. Second, if you think that your GPA is within a respectable range, you should begin applying to unconventional places. Two of the offers that I received were at firms that did not post an articling position. I sought them out first. You may have to do this. Small communities are often an excellent possibility. Sole practitioners in larger centres are also a good possibility. Further, non-profit organizations are also candidates. The key is to approach these individuals, firms and organizations with a real plan. Most of them will need to be guided through the process and made to understand what having an articling student entails. You may find yourself in a situation where you will need to obtain the funding, perhaps along with the organization, for your articling year.

You may want to take a year away from law. You can enjoy one more year of freedom, take a temporary job that you will enjoy, and try again the following summer to find an article. By then, hopefully your GPA and résumé will be stronger.

Another option is to look to more remote communities. Firms in the NWT, Yukon and Nunavut often have a difficult time in filling articling positions. Sometimes the situation is similar in more northern provincial centres as well.

Have your résumé reassessed by a career officer and by colleagues. You might even consider asking for feedback from lawyers that have interviewed you. Approach them with tact, and let them know of your situation. Let them know that feedback from them will be greatly appreciated and will help you to obtain that important articling position. Most, if not all, lawyers will agree to help you. Ask them for constructive criticism. Take it with some humility and try your best to incorporate their comments. You may also want to ask colleagues to do a few mock interviews with you to polish up your interview skills.

The key is to not give up. Apply for all positions that open that are within reason for you and your family, if you have one. Open your mind to all possibilities. I believe that the person who has tenacity and a true desire to succeed will do so.

F. ARE GRADES STILL IMPORTANT?

This may come as a shocker to those who are uninitiated into law school. Except for the select few who don't have an article, or who are in the running for gold, silver or bronze medals, or who plan to do legal graduate school, grades are unimportant in your third year of law school. In fact, there are many jokes that go around amongst articling students and associates regarding the fact. In many, if not most cases, hiring firms do not look at third year marks when they have hired you the previous year. Why should they? You have already proven to them that you are a capable learner, that you have the ability to analyze and apply the law. You have shown your competitiveness, and most important, you have shown your loyalty to the firm by accepting an article with them.

Some of you may be thinking that this is a crazy notion – "What's the use of third year then?" You are not alone in thinking like this. Many third year students are frustrated by this fact. It makes it difficult to remain motivated. You may begin resenting second year students in your class who are diligently taking notes in class, and spending umpteen hours in the law library each day. You may be daydreaming about your upcoming holiday, or be focussed on a new hobby, now that you have some breathing room. Do not feel too bad about this.

For those of you who decide that you want to go on to graduate school, grades will remain very important. It may be even harder for you to remain motivated. However, the fact that many of your classmates in third year will become lackadaisical will be to your advantage when it comes to the bell curve grading. In addition, there will be a small number of people vying for the Dean's list, a very honourable bragging right that you can carry with you for the rest of your career.

Don't forget about learning for intrinsic reasons and not just for someone else. Grades and the evaluation methods used trick us into forgetting that law school is about learning the law!

For those of you who decide to stop caring, consider this: In less than a year's time, you will be entering the practice of law. A Student-at-Law is not expected to know everything that they need to know (in fact, far from it). However, you will be expected to have a minimal level of competency. Further, you will enter preparation for your call to the bar. The more preparation you do in third year, theoretically, the less strenuous your bar ad or CPLED course preparation will be. Some students claim that their classes do not help them to prepare for bar preparation. Others claim that certain classes are imperative, and that doing well in those classes lends itself to success on the bar exam or CPLED courses. The best thing is to ask colleagues who are currently articling and studying for the bar exam what their experience. It will likely depend on your particular law school and its curriculum, and will depend on your particular provincial bar ad course curriculum.

G. CHECK CREDIT AND COURSE REQUIREMENTS

It may seem ludicrous, but students have arrived at their last semester of law school, or even graduation, suddenly realizing that they are short on their credit hours. You may think that this advice does not apply to you, but I suggest that you check and double check and triple check that you will meet your credit requirements well in advance. In fact, be sure before you even begin third year. As well, if you end up having to juggle your schedule, be sure to check again that you have all your credits to graduate. Can you imagine facing your articling principal and asking them to defer your article for another semester so that you can take that one last lousy course to graduate?

This same principle applies to required courses. Many law schools have particular course requirements for upper year students. Be sure that you have scheduled these in, because you cannot graduate without meeting these requirements.

H. HELP OUT THOSE BELOW YOU

The reason that I wrote this book was because I was constantly hoping and wishing for upper year wisdom to flow down to me. On a few rare occasions, I benefited from the kindness of an upper year student. A little hint regarding law school administration, mooting strategies, what courses are most useful, what professors are most enjoyable, what firms are hiring, what firms to avoid, upcoming networking events, exam strategies, and legal discussions are all examples of extremely useful information that can really help out your up-and-coming legal colleagues. You might think of those behind you in their legal studies are competitors that don't require help. However, the more respect that you can show during law school, the more potential opportunity there is to work in harmony post-law school. The law world is a small one, and a good referral or legal source can be extremely valuable to your personal legal career. It is much better to make friends than enemies.

The best thing that you can do for a classmate or a lower year student is to refer them to this book. It will contain most of what they need to know. If the book is missing anything that pertains to your law school or experience, let that person know, and let me know as soon as possible (adam@canadalaw student.ca), so that I can amend the book or website and pass on that valuable information.

I. OPPORTUNITIES FOR NON FACULTY CLASSES

Some Faculties will accommodate one course outside of the Law Faculty in your upper year(s). Consider this option. It can be a great way to take a course that you always wanted to take in your undergraduate studies. Many people choose to take language courses if they think they might face a bilingual situation in their law career. Others take the opportunity to take introductory or brush-up courses in business, especially if they are embarking on a corporate law career.

Most Faculties ask you to provide a brief application, including reasons for taking the out-of-Faculty course, how it will apply to your legal career, and that sort of thing.

J. REGISTER FOR BAR EXAM COURSES / CPLED

Make sure that you do not miss any application deadlines. You do not want to set back your articling start date. Find out these dates far in advance and be sure to get the applications in the mail on time.

K. ARRANGE START DATE FOR YOUR ARTICLE

You might have arranged a start date at the time of your article offer acceptance. If you did not, now is the time to ensure that you have a start date written in stone. See if there is any flexibility on the part of the firm. You might not want to rush into your article. You have just been through three of the hardest years of your life. Many students choose to go on a vacation to Europe or Australia, or some other dream destination. It may be your last chance to do something like this for a while. In any case, give yourself at least a month to wind down, get your living arrangements taken care of, and to make some time for those neglected family members and friends. Or, you may want to begin earlier because you are desperate for an income.

L. 3L EVALUATION

To look backward for a while is to refresh the eye,
to restore it, and to render it the more fit for its
prime function of looking forward.
— Margaret Fairless Barber

You have done it! You have graduated from law school. Way to go! So, now what?

You will usually have a month or two (or sometimes more) to sit back and ponder your three years of law school. Many students take the opportunity to travel, to get away and to regroup before embarking on their articling year. This is a fantastic idea. It is a good idea to get a lot of rest, as the articling year usually proves to be very challenging, mentally, physically and emotionally. Many people say that it is akin to your first year in law school, and by now you will have some very definite memories of that time.

You will want to take stock of what you have learned. Now is a good time to organize all of the notes that you took during the last three years. Organize any important textbooks. If you can, gather up CANS or outlines from courses that you did not have the opportunity to take, as these may help you during your article. If you feel that you need to brush up on some areas that you know you will be involved in, take some time to casually read that material.

You have succeeded through a rite of passage. You are one huge step forward towards becoming a lawyer. Congratulate yourself. Revel in the feeling that you have made it this far. Not many people make it into law school. Even fewer graduate from law school.

Not everything is roses in law school. I think you will have come to that conclusion on your own after reading this book. There are many hurdles to overcome, many routes you can take. There is no right or correct way to become a lawyer in Canada. The adventure is yours to pursue. I hope that you enjoy yourself as much as I have and do. So, you want to be a lawyer, eh? I wish you the very best of luck!

CHAPTER 9:
CONCLUSION &
FINAL THOUGHTS

Again, thank you for buying and reading this book. Please feel free to tell your friends, colleagues and associates about its contents and about how it has helped you to sort through the complex task of becoming a lawyer in Canada. Please respect the copyright existing on the contents of this book and do not pass along the book for free. You may be tempted to do this, especially if you have purchased the electronic copy. Who will ever know, right?

This book is how I am paying off my student loans, so please be honest. I have put hours and hours of time into researching and writing the book. I know that we are all facing a financial crunch because of high tuition and cost of living, but as someone studying and practicing the law, I think you can appreciate the importance of maintaining copyright, and of paying the author for the work contained in this book. Thank you, sincerely, for your consideration.

APPENDICES

A. ALTERNATIVE CAREERS FOR LAWYERS

I have prepared a comprehensive list of alternative legal careers, along with some further information. If you would like a copy of this document, please email me at adam@canadalaw student.ca for a free copy.

B. Law School Admission Information

School	Average LSAT	Average GPA	Weight of LSAT/GPA	# of Applicants	# Admissions	Total Student Body	Yrs Undergrad Required	Application Deadline	Combined Programs	Tuition
UBC	160	82%	50/50	2000	200	630	3	1-Feb	MBA, MAPPS	$9,600.00
U Vic	85-92%	3.7-3.87	30/70	N/A	105	315	3	Feb 1(rolling)	MBA, MPA, MAIG	$8,421.00
U of Alberta	160	3.6	50/50	1200	175	500	3	1-Nov	MBA	$9,434.00
U of Calg	158	3.52	N/A	843	72	N/A	2	1-Feb	MBA, MEDes	$8,300.00
U of Sask	159	3.5	50/50	600-1010	110	N/A	2	1-Feb	N/A	$7,263.00
U of Manitoba	158	3.75	50/50	900-1000	101	N/A	2	1-Feb	MES MBA	$10,000.00
Osgoode Hall	80%	3.65	N/A	1600	215	N/A	2	1-Nov	MBA(MPA), MES	$12,800.00
U of Toronto	165	3.8	N/A	1900	170	525	3	1-Nov	Cert. Enviro Stud., Coll M.A. (Int'l Rel.), M.A. (Crim, Econ, Russ. & East Euro Stud.), M.B.A., M.I.St., M.S.W., Ph.D. (Econ, Phil, Poli-Sci)	$16,800.00
Queen's	159	79.00%	50/50		160	N/A	2	1-Nov	MIR, MPA, Civil	$12,856.00
Western	160	3.7	50/50	2400	160-165	N/A	3	1-Nov	MBA, HBA, MIT	$10,624.00
Windsor	N/A	N/A	N/A	1600	N/A	N/A	N/A	3-Nov	JD, MBA,	$9,263.00
U of Ottawa	156	80%	N/A	2700	152	717	2	1-Nov	LLL, MBA, JD, MA (Int'l Affrs),	$8,912.00
McGill	160	3.7	N/A	1700	170	N/A	2	15-Jan	BCL, MBA, MSW	$3036-$5951
U of New Brunswick	159	3.7	40/60	920	80	230	3	1-Mar	MBA	$6,972.00
Dalhousie	81%	3.3	60/40	N/A	155	N/A	3	28-Feb	MBA, MPA, MLIS, MHSA	$10,577.00
U of Moncton	N/A	3.3	N/A	N/A	55	N/A	3	30-Apr	N/A	N/A

C. SAMPLE COVER LETTERS AND SAMPLE RÉSUMÉ

Please note that I include my own personal information within these samples. I do so not to make myself look good, or because I think they are the ultimate samples. They are simply what I have available to me, and I did not want to make one up. It was a lot easier to just leave them as is and allow you to customize them for your own needs. Further, they worked very well for me.

Sample Cover Letter #1:

> 55555 55 Avenue Edmonton, AB T63 4B3
> (780) 555-5555 XXXX@ualberta.ca
> www.AdamLetourneau.com

May 3, 2004

Fraser Milner Casgrain LLP
30th Floor, Fifth Avenue Place
237 - 4th Avenue S.W.
Calgary, Alberta T2P 4X7

Dear Mr. X,

Mr. Y of ABC and Mr. W and Mr. M of Fraser Milner Casgrain LLP, all of whom I met last summer during my time at ABC Legal Services suggested that I contact you to discuss the possibility of an articling position with your firm. I am currently enrolled in the Faculty of Law at the University of Alberta and will graduate in May 2005. I am applying for an articling position at Fraser Milner Casgrain LLP for the 2005-06 term. I am particularly interested in Corporate/Commercial Law, Intellectual Property & Technology, although I also have other interests.

I am extremely disciplined, I have excellent time management skills and I am accustomed to setting goals and working hard to achieve them. As my résumé indicates, I have experience in successfully managing and developing companies, along with advanced expertise in publishing, computer programming and Internet technology. Recently, I helped to launch an electronic publishing company. I have also assisted in the start up of a publishing house, a youth magazine, a web design and editing company, an online liquidation company and an online shopping website. I am a published editor and writer, and have first-class research and writing skills.

My summer employment at ABC Legal Services has provided me with valuable legal insight and my experience as Co-Editor-in-Chief of the Alberta Law Review will undoubtedly familiarize me with interesting and diverse legal issues. Further, my participation in the Kawaskhimon National Aboriginal Moot has honed my oral and written advocacy skills.

I hold B.Sc. and B.A. degrees, speak and read French at an intermediate level and come from Métis background. I have been very involved in volunteer activities, most recently with the Alberta Law Review (Co-Editor-in-Chief), Aboriginal Law Students Association (President), Club Tout Droit (President), and the Oratory Association. The website I have designed(www.AdamLetourneau.com) elaborates on my skills, experience and extra-curricular interests.

I would be very pleased to meet with you to discuss the possibility of articling with your firm. I can be reached at (780) 555-5555 or XXXXX@ualberta.ca.

Yours faithfully,

Adam Letourneau
Enclosures: résumé, references, transcripts

Sample Cover Letter #2

55555 55 Avenue Edmonton, AB T63 4B3
(780) 555-5555 XXXX@ualberta.ca
www.AdamLetourneau.com

May 4, 2004

Ms. X
Justice Canada
211 - 10199 - 101 Street
Edmonton, AB T5J 3Y4

Dear Ms. X,

I am applying for an articling position with Justice Canada for the
2005-2006 term. I am Métis and I attend the Faculty of Law at the
University of Alberta. I will graduate in June 2005. I am particularly
interested in Litigation, Intellectual Property & Technology,
International Law, and Aboriginal Law, although I also have other
interests.

I am extremely disciplined, I have excellent time management skills
and I am accustomed to setting goals and working hard to achieve
them. As my résumé indicates, I have experience in successfully
managing and developing companies, along with advanced expertise
in publishing, computer programming and Internet technology.
Recently, I helped to launch an electronic publishing company. I have
also assisted in the start up of a publishing house, a youth magazine, a
web design and editing company, an online liquidation company and
an online shopping website. I am a published editor and writer, and
have first-class research and writing skills.

My summer employment at ABC Legal Services has provided me
with valuable legal insight and my experience as Co-Editor-in-Chief
of the Alberta Law Review this year will undoubtedly familiarize me
with interesting and diverse legal issues. Further, my participation in
the Kawaskhimon National Aboriginal Moot has honed my oral and
written advocacy skills.

I hold B.Sc. and B.A. degrees, speak and read French at an intermediate level, and Edmonton is where my family, and extended family call home. I have been very involved in volunteer activities, most recently with the Alberta Law Review (Co-Editor-in-Chief), Aboriginal Law Students Association (President), and Club Tout Droit (President). The website I have designed (www.AdamLetourneau.com) elaborates on my skills, experience and extra-curricular interests.

I would be very pleased to meet with you to discuss the possibility of articling with Justice Canada. I can be reached at (780) 555-5555 or XXXX@ualberta.ca.

Yours faithfully,

Adam Letourneau
Enclosures: résumé, references, transcripts; further reference letters to follow directly from referees

Sample Résumé #1:

Note that this entire résumé fits on two 8.5 x 11 inch sheets. It is compressed and somewhat modified here due to page size limitations. You should aim to have your résumé fit on two pages as well.

Adam O. Letourneau
55555 55 Avenue, Edmonton, AB, Canada T63 4BY
Phone: (780) 555-5555 Email: XXXXX@ualberta.ca

EDUCATION

2005	**Bachelor of Laws,** University of Alberta
2002	**Bachelor of Arts, English,** Athabasca University
1997	**Bachelor of Science, Psychology,** University of Calgary
1992~1995	Advanced French - Université du Québec à Trois-Rivières, Summer 1995 - Collège de Bois de Boulogne, Summer 1992

WORK EXPERIENCE

2004	**Co-Editor-in-Chief,** Alberta Law Review * Coordinate quarterly publication of legal academic journal, including management of 30 editors and various committees; Perform chief edits on all articles.
2003	**Summer Student,** Petro-Canada Legal Services Department * Assisted 16 in-house lawyers with various legal issues, including contract, commercial, environmental, insurance, employment, aboriginal and other areas of law.

2000   **Vice President, Operations,** PublicationsUnbound, Inc.
~2002   * Supervised up to 9 staff and 20 contractors. Managed
            ~150 strategic partners. Directed all web site development
            and maintenance (50+ websites). Created strategic plans for
            eCommerce and distribution of 3000 eBooks via the
            Internet through a proprietary syndicated network.
            Coordinated exclusive launch with Amazon.com.

2000   **President / Founder,** OlenInc.
~2003   * Web development and editing firm. Designed created
            small to mid-sized web sites, edited three Masters theses
            (one LLM, one MBA, one MSc), various editing services.

1999   **Vice President, Editing Operations,** American Book
~2000   Publishing Group
            * Large publishing house. Managed group of 67 editors.

1999   **Vice President / Principal,** aShoppingGuide.com
~2000   * Managed 10 employees and 22 contractors, directed all
            web marketing and site promotion, community
            development, site co-branding, strategic partnerships,
            merchant and affiliate management. Supervised all web site
            design and layout.

1999   **Director of Communications,** LiquidationShop.com
            * Directed and designed communication and business
            initiatives for start-up company.

1998   **Associate Editor / Event Programmer,** The Canadian
~1999   Parking Association
            * Trade Magazine. Programmed annual national conferences
            & bi-annual world symposium.

ACHIEVEMENTS

- Member of the Kawaskihmon National Aboriginal moot team
  (2004)
- Elected Editor-in-Chief of the Alberta Law Review (2004)

AWARDS

- Encana Corporation Scholarship (2003 and 2004)
- Faculty of Law Aboriginal Law Bursary (2004)
- TransAlta Education Award (2003 and 2004)
- Roger Carter Scholarship (2004)
- Belcourt Brosseau Métis Award (2003 and 2004)
- Peter Freeman QC Bursary for Indigenous Students in Law (2003)
- Justice Canada Legal Studies for Aboriginal People Program Bursary (2002, 2003, 2004)
- Honours Academic Scholarship; Leadership Scholarship; Outstanding Achievement Scholarship (1992-1993)
- Crescent Heights High School - Ruthorford Scholarship; Citizen of the Year Award; First Class Honours Award; Physical Education Award (1992)

ASSOCIATIONS

- Canadian Bar Association
- Indigenous Bar Association
- U of A Native Student Association

VOLUNTEER

- 2003~2005   Alberta Law Review Editorial Board
- 2003~2004   Club Tout Droit – President
- 2004~2005   University of Alberta Graduation Pow Wow

  Steering Committee
- 2002~2005   Aboriginal Law Students' Association – Treasurer then President
- 2002~2004   Faculty of Law Oratory Association – Technical Director
- 2003~2004   Advisory Committee Member Indigenous Law Program
- 2002~2004   Cannons of Construction (Law

School Newspaper) – Editor, Writer
- 2002~2003   Student Legal Services - Criminal Project; Civil Law Project
- 2003   Philip C. Jessup International Law Moot Court Competition Volunteer
- 2002   Calgary Mountain Bike Alliance – Trail Maintenance Leader
- 2001   U of C Native Centre - Resident Tech Head
- 2001~2002   Venturer Group – NW Calgary – Scoutmaster
- 1999~2000   goMagazine Inc. - Contributing Editor
- 1998~1999   Fast Company Magazine - Cell Coordinator

COMPUTER COMPETENCY

Expert skill with many computer applications, web design, programming, desktop publishing, and electronic publishing. Exceptional on-line research skills, including QuickLaw and eCarswell.

LEISURE & INTERESTS

Triathlon, golf, hiking, yoga, Canadian and children's literature, my 3 children.

D. Sample Statements of Interest

Both of these sample interest statement letters resulted in acceptance to three or more Canadian law schools. Use them as a reference, but do not copy them. Make your Statement of Interest your own. Make it interesting.

In preparing my Statement of Interest letter, I relied upon the information provided at http://www.accepted.com/mba/dodonts.aspx.

It is aimed towards MBA students, but is equally applicable to prospective law students.

Statement of Interest – Adam Letourneau

I'm not supposed to be writing a Statement of Interest for an application to the University of Alberta Faculty of Law. I'm supposed to be *maintaining* the status quo. I'm supposed to be negotiating a higher salary and more stock options at my next quarterly review. I'm supposed to be thinking of ways to make the company more efficient, more effective.

However, here I am writing it nonetheless. I am writing it because it is important to me. It is important because it will pass the rocking chair test.

Some friends and I belong to a little group that we call "The Rocking Chair Test Club". It's simple – it goes like this: "When I am sitting on the front porch of my house, rocking in my favourite chair, my trusty dog by my side, will I remember what I am doing today and smile?"

One of my favourite test subjects was a weeklong trip to California and Mexico. In a whirling week, I experienced ocean, surf, sand, cities, desert and adventure! On an absolute shoe-string budget, I lived life to its fullest. No regrets and no self-imposed limitations.

I think that Law School *will* be like this for me. When I am old and grey, I will consider the challenge, the diversity and the opportunity to do something great! I have friends in Law School and they are "living it". They are creating memories with their fellow classmates and professors. They are exploring the complex subtleties of the law and are preparing themselves for a long series of voyages. I want to be there too.

I am applying to participate in the joint LL.B/MBA Programme. Although my diverse work experience, along with my educational, cultural and volunteer background have provided me with a plethora of learning opportunities, I am ready for a new challenge – a big challenge. One that will influence who I become and what direction my life will take, and I believe that the University of Alberta can offer this. I attended the U of C for two years, completing my B.Sc. and enjoyed it immensely. There is nothing that I would rather do than stay in Alberta, a true province of adventure.

I have had the opportunity to be involved in a number of start-up businesses over the last six years. In various roles, with most of them at an executive level, I learned what it takes to rise up to a challenge. Bringing to fruition an idea or concept is arduous, risky work. Many times have I experienced defeat when trying to "make it happen", but so far I have not lost the battle, and I do not intend to. I have assisted fine colleagues in creating an online auction house, a full-fledged publishing house, a magazine, and an electronic publishing distribution company, not to mention the many small projects that I have been involved in. I have also been able to establish a number of mentoring relationships, being both mentor and mentoree. These relationships have been invaluable in shaping my business aspirations and my career goals and objectives. As well, I have been able to help a number of young people to find direction in their lives. This is extremely rewarding!

I have supported myself since high school and have fully funded both of my undergraduate degrees. I have also supported my wife and two children in recent years. I have always had to work full-time or close to full-time while attending school. I am in decent financial shape currently, but will require financial assistance in order to attend Law School this September. I have faith that the funds will be there when required.

Subsequently, I have so much to offer the University of Alberta Faculty of Law. I bring leadership, astute research skills, a keen interest in thoughtful discussion and dialogue, and a passionate yearning to learn. I have an interesting background, with Cree, French and Swedish traditions to draw from. I thrive on sport competition and have immersed myself in the world of writing and publishing. I am a self-taught 'techie' and a well-mentored business diplomat. I am also an avid member of the community at large, and an active member of the First Nation community. I look forward to honing these skills within the walls of the University of Alberta.

I have a keen interest in learning about all areas of Law, but particular curiosity about the areas of Corporate Law, Environmental Law and Aboriginal Law. There is so much to learn, and so many opportunities to apply that knowledge in practical ways.

If I am selected from among your excellent pool of applicants, I can assure you with confidence that I will bring a level of merit and achievement unsurpassed. I am writing this Statement for one reason only – for the opportunity to pass the rocking chair test of all rocking chair tests.

I strongly urge the Admissions Committee to consider my application.

Adam Letourneau

Statement of Interest – Mark Anthony (Names and Places Changed)

I will not be satisfied until I hear the words "Congratulations on being called to the Bar of Saskatchewan 2004!" If it were possible for the Faculty of Law to represent on indices an applicant's sheer desire to undertake LL.B. studies, it is a certainty that you would find the name Mark Anthony in the upper-echelon of all applicants. I have completed a B.A., a B.Sc., and I will complete an M.Sc. next year. I have worked for the Congolese government as a civil servant since September 1996, garnering knowledge of Congolese language, culture, customs, education and business. Recently, I was offered an English teaching position at a top-tier U.S. university for the April 2000 session. I deliberated whether to accept this position vis-à-vis attending law school. I declined the job offer because I am most compelled to undertake LL.B. studies.

I have great concerns about the environment, as well as the welfare of handicapped and aged persons. I am passionately involved in volunteer activities related to these causes. Completing an LL.B. degree would provide me with the tools necessary to lobby for societal change and make positive contributions to the field of law. Law School also interests me because undertaking LL.B. studies would place me in a veritably challenging environment. I need to be challenged.

As an undergraduate B.A. student at the University of Saskatchewan, I often pondered how rewarding LL.B. studies would be. I am drawn to attend law school at the University of Saskatchewan due to the low student-professor ratio and the increasingly positive reputation of the program. In addition, I will return to Saskatoon (from the Congo) in August of 2000, after having been away from my family and friends for more than 3 years. Acceptance into the University of Saskatchewan's Faculty of Law would make my homecoming even more special.

The thought of attending law school has long pervaded my thoughts. As I approach age 26, having completed two undergraduate degrees and working toward completion of an M.Sc., I know I now have the personal and academic maturity necessary to excel in my studies. If I am selected to attend law school at the University of Saskatchewan, I will undertake a leadership role in the Faculty of Law and I will be an active contributor to the community.

I strongly urge the Admissions Committee not to overlook my application.

Sincerely,

Mark Anthony

E. LAW LINKS

a. **www.canadalawstudent.ca** – where you can buy this book, and where you can get updated Canadian law student information beyond what this book has to offer.

b. Canadian Law Schools - **http://www.geocities.com/canadianlawschools/** - brief information for the interested law student. Also includes a discussion board.

c. Canadian Law Schools Forum - **http://p210.ezboard.com/bcanadianlawschools**.

d. First year Student Bookshelf (WestlaweCarswell) - **http://www.westlawecarswell.com/lawschool/firstyear.htm**.

e. Canadian Law Schools - A resource for prospective law students, created by the Council of Canadian Law Deans (CCLD). **http://www.canadalawschools.ca/**.

f. Getting into Canadian law schools – Campusaccess - **http://www.campusaccess.com/campus_web/educ/e4grad_lacan.htm**.

g. Firm Salaries & Other Statistics Charts **http://www.infirmation.com/shared/insider/payscale.tcl?state=international**.

h. National Magazine **http://www.cba.org/CBA/National/students/**

i. Find more links at **www.canadalawstudent.ca**.

F. Law Schools in Canada

BRITISH COLUMBIA

University of British Columbia - Faculty of Law, 1822 East Mall, Vancouver, British Columbia, V6T 1Z1,Tel: (604) 822-2818, Fax: (604) 822-4781, http://www.law.ubc.ca/, LL.B. / Combined Program Admissions Inquiries: borthwick@law.ubc.ca, Graduate Student Admissions Inquiries: graduates@law.ubc.ca..

University of Victoria - Faculty of Law, P.O. Box 2400, Victoria, British Columbia, V8W 3H7, Tel: (250) 721-8147, Fax: (250) 472-4299 or (250) 721-6390, http://www.law.uvic.ca/, Admissions Office: lawadmss@uvic.ca.

ALBERTA

University of Alberta - Faculty of Law, 485 Law Centre, University of Alberta, Edmonton, Alberta, T6G 2H5, Tel: (780) 492-5590, Fax: (780) 492-4924, http://www.law.ualberta.ca/, Admissions: kjwilson@law.ualberta.ca.

The University of Calgary - Faculty of Law, 2500 University Drive, N.W. Calgary, Alberta, T2N 1N4, Tel: (403) 220-7116, Fax: (403) 282-8325, http://www.law.ucalgary.ca/, law@ucalgary.ca.

SASKATCHEWAN

University of Saskatchewan - College of Law, 15 Campus Drive, Saskatoon, Saskatchewan, S7N 5A6, Tel: (306) 966-5910, Fax: (306) 966-5900, http://www.usask.ca/law/, law_admissions@usask.ca.

MANITOBA

University of Manitoba - Faculty of Law, Room 301, Robson Hall, Winnipeg, Manitoba, R3T 2N2, Tel: (204) 474-9282, Fax: (204) 474-7580
http://www.umanitoba.ca/faculties/law/newsite/index.php, UM-LAW@cc.umanitoba.ca.

ONTARIO

Carleton University - Department of Law, C473 Loeb Building, 1125 Colonel By Drive, Ottawa, Ontario, K1S 5B6, Tel: (613) 520-2600, Ext. 8212, Fax: (613) 520-4467, http://www.carleton.ca/law/index.html, law@carleton.ca.

York University - Osgoode Hall Law School, 4700 Keele Street, North York, Ontario, M3J 1P3, Tel: (416) 736-5199, Fax: (416) 736-5251, http://www.osgoode.yorku.ca/.

Queen's University - Faculty of Law, Macdonald Hall, Kingston, Ontario, K7L 3N6, Tel: (613) 533-6000, ext. 74285, Fax: (613) 533-6509, http://law.queensu.ca/index.php.

University of Ottawa - Faculty of Law, Common Law Section, 57 Louis Pasteur, Ottawa, Ontario, K1N 6N5, Tel: (613) 562-5927, Fax: (613) 562-5124, http://www.commonlaw.uottawa.ca/eng/index.htm.

Université d'Ottawa- Faculté de droit, Section de droit civil, 57 Louis Pasteur, Ottawa, Ontario, K1N 6N5, Tel: (613) 562-

5902, Fax: (613) 562-512,
http://www.commonlaw.uottawa.ca/fra/index.htm.

University of Toronto - Faculty of Law, 84 Queen's Park,
Toronto, Ontario, M5S 2C5, Tel: (416) 978-3718, Fax: (416)
971-3026, http://www.law.utoronto.ca/,
law.admissions@utoronto.ca.

University of Western Ontario - Faculty of Law, London,
Ontario, N6A 3K7, Tel: (519) 661-3346, Fax: (519) 850-2412,
http://www.law.uwo.ca/mainSite/.

University of Windsor - Faculty of Law, 401 Sunset Avenue,
Windsor, Ontario, N9B 3P4, Tel: (519) 253-4232, Ext. 2930,
Fax: (519) 973-7064, http://athena.uwindsor.ca/law.

QUÉBEC

Université Laval- Faculté de droit, Pavillon CharlesDeKoninck,
Québec, Québec, G1K 7P4, Tel: (418) 656-3511, Fax: (418)
656-7714, http://www.fd.ulaval.ca/.

McGill University - Faculty of Law, 3644 Peel Street, Montréal,
Québec, H3A 1W9, Tel: (514) 398-6604, Fax: (514) 398-4659,
http://www.law.mcgill.ca/, info.law@mcgill.ca.

Université de Montréal - Faculté de droit, C. P. 6128,
succursale Centre-Ville, Montréal, Québec, H3C 3J7, Tel: (514)
343-2356, Fax: (514) 343-2199,
http://www2.droit.umontreal.ca.

Université du Québec à Montréal - Département des sciences
juridiques, C.P. 8888, succursale Centre-ville, Montréal,
Québec, H3C 3P8, Tel: (514) 987-3000, ext. 7047, Fax: (514)
987-4784, http://www.juris.uqam.ca/.

Université de Sherbrooke - Faculté de droit, 2500 boul. Université, Sherbrooke, Québec, J1K 2R1, Tel: (819) 821-7511, Fax: (819) 821-7578, http://www.usherbrooke.ca/droit/.

NEW BRUNSWICK

University of New Brunswick - Faculty of Law, Ludlow Hall, Box 4400, Fredericton, New Brunswick, E3B 5A3, Tel: (506) 453-4702, Fax: (506) 453-4604, http://law.unb.ca/, warbeau@unb.ca.

Université de Moncton - École de droit, Université de Moncton, New Brunswick, E1A 3E9, Tel: (506) 858-3705, Fax: (506) 858-4534, http://www3.umoncton.ca/UdeM_menu1.cfm?www=http://www3.umoncton.ca/cdem/droit/.

NOVA SCOTIA

Dalhousie University - Dalhousie Law School, 6061 University Avenue, Halifax, Nova Scotia, B3H 4H9, Tel: (902) 494-2114, Fax: (902) 494-1316, http://as01.ucis.dal.ca/law/index.html, Law.admissions@dal.ca.

ABOUT THE AUTHOR

Adam O. Letourneau earned a Bachelor of Science in Psychology from the University of Calgary in 1997. He then undertook a career in business, technology and publishing, gaining valuable experience in business start-ups and executive management. In addition to working on other ventures, Letourneau acted as Vice President of Operations of a high-tech/publishing company in Calgary, and before that as Vice President, Editing Operations of a publishing house in the United States. While working in business, Letourneau earned a Bachelor of Arts in English from Athabasca University in 2002. Letourneau earned a Bachelor of Laws from the University of Alberta in 2005. While at the University of Alberta, he was elected as Editor-in-Chief of the *Alberta Law Review*, as President of the Aboriginal Law Students' Association and as President of the Law Faculty French Club. He also worked for the Centre for Constitutional Studies. Letourneau is currently completing his law articles at North & Company LLP. He is presently on the Board of Directors of Apeetogosan (Metis) Development Inc. and the Lethbridge Humane Society. In his spare time, Letourneau enjoys cycling, fishing and gardening. Letourneau and his wife, Carmen, have two daughters, Zoë Skye and Soleil Rhiannon and have a son, Zane Olen.

Submissions

If you have a book manuscript that you would like published, visit www.writingonstone.ca for submission guidelines. Writing on Stone Press accepts unsolicited manuscripts for a variety of topics for publication.